MY FAMILY FINANCIAL MIRACLE

A New Way of Thinking to Protect and Control Your Money

Dr. Nelson P. Rivers

Centennial Wealth
Promo Code: 000367
Phone: (812) 491-3765

MY FAMILY FINANCIAL MIRACLE

A New Way of Thinking to Protect and Control Your Money

Merle Gilley

Hugo House

My Family Financial Miracle: A New Way of Thinking to Protect and Control Your Money

ISBN: 978-1-936449-70-5

Library of Congress Control Number: 2015940333

Trademark Information
The "S&P 500" and the "Dow Jones Industrial Average" are products of S&P Dow Jones Indices LLC ("SPDJI"). Standard & Poor's®, S&P® and S&P 500® are registered trademarks of Standard & Poor's Financial Services LLC ("S&P"); DJIA®, The Dow®, Dow Jones® and Dow Jones Industrial Average are trademarks of Dow Jones Trademark Holdings LLC ("Dow Jones"); and these trademarks have been licensed for use by SPDJI.

This book is not sponsored, endorsed, sold or promoted by SPDJI, Dow Jones, S&P, their respective affiliates, and none of such parties make any representation regarding the advisability of investing in such product(s) nor do they have any liability for any errors, omissions, or interruptions of the S&P 500 or the Dow Jones Industrial Average.

Cover Design: Mark Patterson, www.theBrandArtist.com

Interior Layout: Ronda Taylor, www.taylorbydesign.com

Hugo House Publishers, Ltd.
Denver, Colorado
Austin, Texas
www.HugoHousePublishers.com

Limits of Liability

The author and publisher shall not be liable for misuse of this material. This book is strictly for informational and educational purposes.

Disclaimer

While great efforts have been taken to provide accurate and current information regarding the covered material, neither the author, MFFM, LLC, or any affiliates are responsible for any errors or omissions, or for the results or lack of results obtained from the use of this information.

Every effort has been made to accurately represent these products and their potential. However, there is no guarantee that you will earn any money using the techniques and ideas in these materials. Examples in these materials are not to be interpreted as a promise or guarantee of earnings. Earning potential is entirely dependent on the person using our product, ideas and techniques. We do not purport this as a "get rich scheme."

Your level of success in attaining the results claimed in our materials depends on the time you devote to the program, ideas and techniques mentioned, your finances, knowledge and various skills. Since these factors differ according to individuals, we cannot guarantee your success or income level, nor are we responsible for any of your actions.

Materials in our products may contain information that includes or is based upon forward-looking statements. Any and all forward-looking statements here or on any of our material are intended to express our opinion of earnings potential. Many factors will be important in determining your actual results and no guarantees are made that you will achieve results similar to ours or anybody else's; in fact no guarantees are made that you will achieve any results from our ideas and techniques in our material.

The ideas, suggestions, general principles and conclusions presented here are subject to local, state and federal laws and regulations and revisions of same, and are intended for informational purposes only. All information in *My Family Financial Miracle* is provided "as is," with no guarantee of completeness, accuracy, or timeliness regarding the results obtained from the use of this information.

The permanent life insurance products discussed in this book are not stock market investments. They do not directly participate in any stock or equity investments and do not receive dividend or capital gains participation. They are insurance policies that have accumulation accounts linked to a financial index. Their performance varies based on the product used, method of funding, size of policy and performance of an index; past index performance is no indication of future crediting rates. All life insurance policies have sales charges, maintenance fees and the cost of insurance. Interest crediting fluctuations can lead to the need for additional premium in a life insurance policy. All permanent life insurance products should be reviewed with a competent and licensed financial services professional before they are purchased.

Dedication

To my daughter, Mia. You are my inspiration. You provide clarity in my mission to help our young people accomplish their greatest dreams.

Contents

How to Use This Book

This book is meant to be interactive. Throughout the book, you will discover special links that will take you to private webpages where you can access additional information on certain topics I discuss in the book.

The first time you visit this website, you will be asked to input your name and email address. If you have received this book from one of our certified Family Financial Miracle Representatives, be certain to use their private promo code when inputting your information.

Once you sign into the private Family Financial Miracle video page (www.MyFamilyFinancialMiracle.com/video) you will be sent a private link via email that you can use to view any of the videos in the book. Please bookmark this webpage link so you don't have to enter your information more than once.

Let's Connect!

Most important—I want to connect with you and understand what you are thinking. Having a better picture of the specific challenges you face with My Family Financial Miracle, I am better able to serve you through the information I provide. There are a couple of ways that you can reach out and connect with me directly. If you need clarification as you read through my book, if you want to ask questions, if you need advice or clarification, please reach out:

You can email me at info@myfamilyfinancialmiracle.com.

You can connect with me on Facebook at http://facebook.com/myfamilyfinancialmiracle.

You can also visit www.FFMRegistry.com. There you will find a registry of Family Financial Miracle Representatives whom you can contact in your local area for more information as well.

As you will see in this book, the information I am giving you comes from long experience and a deep desire to help people handle their family finances in the most effective ways by helping you understand how to grow your money in a protected environment that allows you income through liquidity, use, and control.

I wish you well in your financial journey.

Sincerely,

Merle Gilley

Prologue

I'm frustrated. The financial information that is available to the average American consumer is not shedding light on something that is remarkably helpful for families. However, I found that something, and it not only keeps my money protected but my family too.

As I watch the financial wizards on the television, I think to myself, there really isn't a perfect financial product. But the reason I wrote this book is to show you what I discovered so that, hopefully, you can have the same peace of mind that I have about my family and my money.

There's a reason why I feel so strongly about this. I grew up barely getting by. At one point, I lived in my grandfather's garage with my mom and my little sister. I thought it was a big adventure at the time, and it took my mind off the fact that my dad was off in Vietnam fighting for something I really didn't understand. While he was there, he took up drinking and never was around much after that. My mom was tough. She grew up on a farm in North Carolina, and her parents taught her how to be self-sufficient. She taught me the same. Because I was on my own a lot as a kid, I learned that if I needed something done, I better do it myself.

When I got out of the Air Force, then met and married my wife, she wanted to start a sign company. We took that plunge and started the whole thing out of our kitchen. The ability to get things done for myself helped me run a successful business with my wife. It has helped me be even more successful as a financial strategist. We sold the business, and what I am about to share with you is the fruits of fifteen years of figuring out what to do with the money we made from that sale, solutions that don't risk it, that keep it growing in an environment where it shows decent returns but it never loses any either, so that when I need it, I have it and can use it as I see fit.

You might at first decide to dismiss what I'm going to show you because the guys (and gals) on TV tell you exactly the opposite of what I am about the share with you. Keep in mind that when the stock market crash of 2008-09 happened, the T.V. guru strategies collapsed. I'm not a T.V. financial celebrity, but when the market crashed, I didn't lose any money and neither did my clients.

I don't like that people lose their hard-earned savings because they either get sketchy investment advice or they just simply don't know what to do differently than put their money into a 401(k) and hope and pray it will be enough.

My clients know I care about them, and because of it I have found myself in some very interesting situations. I have had them call me before they call their family when their loved-one passes away. They come to me for advice about how to handle an irresponsible or incapable sibling that is to receive a portion of their parent's inheritance, but the responsible sibling wants to make sure Mom and Dad's money isn't squandered away.

I love it when I can help someone's mother handle whatever life savings she has left, and it pains me when I can't help someone because they have made bad investment decisions or are not handling their money in a way that will truly benefit them. But I have developed a thick skin, and the lessons from my youth come through in the advice I give. You have to be self-sufficient. Relying on someone's advice without doing your homework can lead you down all sorts of rabbit holes that can hurt you.

I wrote this book to clear up some of the myths and misconceptions about retirement savings as well as to show you what can shield it from the risks that threaten to decimate it. I feel strongly enough about this that in the pages that follow, I am going to show you how my financial plan works using my own information. Very few financial experts have the courage to show you their plan and how well—or not—they've done over the past twenty years with their strategies.

I don't want you to worry about something you really don't have to, your money. The retirement vehicle that I found really can save you heartache and headache. It worked so well that I decided to get in the business after I saw what it can do for my money. It is a miracle that can and does happen every day not just for me but for a growing number of Americans just like you who are tired of waking up and finding they don't have enough to live on when they cannot or do not want to work anymore.

I no longer live hand to mouth. I am proud to say that I provide a very comfortable living for my family—something my wife and daughter appreciate very much. I want you to have that comfort as well. Please take what I have to say in these pages and apply it to your life, for this is the only way you can know with certainty that your family financial miracle is there, waiting for you to enjoy.

1 Sink or Swim

What if your boss walked up to you one day and said, "You know what Joe (or Jane)? You have been such a good employee, I want to ensure I have your loyalty until you retire. To do that, I have calculated how much you're going to make at your current salary, $65,000 per year, over the next twenty years. It comes to $1.3 million; I'm going to write you a check for that exact amount. In exchange, I expect you to come to work every day, do the same excellent job you've been doing for me for the past ten years. The only difference is you're getting all your money upfront."

After you got over the shock, you would have to figure out how you would manage all that money. After you paid your taxes on it, you would probably think about paying off your mortgage, putting some in the bank in CDs or money market certificates, and then investing the rest in some sort of mutual fund so you could make some more money—you know, grow your nest egg.

In the year 2000, when I was forty years old, I sold the business my wife, Monica, and I had built for half a million dollars. We started the company when we first got married and grew it into a successful venture over the course of sixteen years. She's a designer; I can build anything, so we built signs. When we handed the keys over to the new owner, we were proud that we could count the US Department of Defense, Dollar Tree, and Papco Oil as clients. In essence, I had just had my employer hand me a check for $500,000. After taxes and broker fees were paid, I was left with about $450,000. It seemed like a fortune at the time.

After the excitement of selling the company wore off, the reality of not having all of the benefits it provided became a reality. This was a time of anxiety. I had a new baby girl, and Monica—my wife and business partner for sixteen years—was now dedicated to staying home until our baby girl was grown. Basically I had just sold the financial vehicle in which we had safeguarded our savings. I felt like we had just put a price tag on our livelihood, had something we had counted on day in, day out for years to provide a comfortable and rewarding lifestyle. But I had to come to terms with the facts: once I sold the company, I traded a safe and predictable livelihood that provided a comfortable lifestyle that I controlled for sixteen years for a bank account full of money.

It is hard for me to put into words the incredible emotions I was experiencing in those days. The best way I can describe it is by telling you a story about how I learned to swim.

When I was five years old I lived in Rhode Island. I lived in a lot of places as a kid because my dad was a Navy Seabee, the U.S. Naval Construction Force. They build everything the Navy needs. One morning my dad asked me if I wanted to go to work with him because he had just finished his latest assignment, the Officers' Club swimming pool. I was so excited. Not only could I spend the day at the pool while he worked, I was going to work with my dad! It didn't matter that I had never been swimming.

When we got to the pool, it was nothing like I had imagined. There was no one there, no adults, no other kids, no one. The pool was gigantic, about the size of a football field, with three diving boards at the far end stacked on top of each other. The water was an inviting sky blue because of the color of the bottom, but as I reached down to feel the temperature of the water with my hand it was cold.

I could tell my dad was feeling proud he was able to provide me access to such a treat. His son was swimming in the same pool the U.S. Navy Officers would use. I was excited but also scared to death because I knew that the water in the shallow end was going to be over my head. I had never been in water over my head.

Dad told me to go in the bath house and put on my bathing suit. The concrete floor was cold on my bare feet, and I wore nothing but my swimming trunks. I was cold, getting colder, and it didn't help that it was a cloudy day.

My dad went into the locker room of the pool house and came out with a life vest. He helped me strap it on, and I remember it being really big. It was brand new, so it was still bright orange. It was also stiff and itchy, and as my dad pulled the straps tight around the front of the vest, I became downright apprehensive. It was huge on me, and no matter how tight my dad pulled the straps, it still flapped.

All that excitement I had about going to work with my dad was gone; all the anticipation about going swimming turned into survival mode. I felt like my dad was preparing me for something I really didn't want to do, but I couldn't allow my dad to think I was not thankful for him bringing me along to work and allowing me access to something this special. If I complained or demanded to go home, he might not ever do it again. So I braced myself, knowing that I was going to swim in this huge, deep, cold swimming pool, all by myself, wearing a life vest that didn't fit.

Dad led me by the hand to the diving boards and ordered me to climb up to the high one. He followed me up the ladder and out onto the board. I felt more and more trapped, but I knew there was no way out. As we walked to the end of that cold sandpapery board, he unceremoniously scooped me up and tossed me off the end. It happened so quickly, I didn't have time to protest. I don't even remember being scared of the height. I do remember hitting the cold water, butt first, and then sinking down—deep, deeper than I definitely felt comfortable with. The life preserver, thankfully, did its job. I eventually bobbed up to the top of the water, face up. I was looking straight up at a cloudy sky, and I could see my dad standing on the end of the diving board above.

He started yelling down to me, "Roll over, kick your feet, and start pulling with your arms."

As I watched him spin his arms around, I thought, "I'm a goner." I know he had no idea how impossible all that was to do. First of all the vest I had on was for a two-hundred pound man. I weighed maybe sixty. Second, the strap that held it to my body was so loose, the only thing keeping me from falling out of the thing was my head was bigger than the hole it was stuck through.

I tried with every muscle in me to flip over. A lady lifeguard came into the pool area as this was all going on and asked my dad if everything was alright. He said, "Yes, I'm teaching my son how to swim."

She went about her business, and my heart sank. All I could think was, "Hey lady I'm drowning over here. Save me!"

It probably took about fifteen minutes—a long, scary quarter of an hour—to reach the side of the pool, me kicking my legs frantically and flailing my arms as my body hung vertically in the water. I was exhausted when I reached the side.

When I got over the euphoria of selling my company for so much money, I felt pretty much the same as I felt that day in the U.S. Navy Officers' Club swimming pool. I knew I was safe in that pool as long as I had that preserver around my neck and my dad close by. But I remember how trapped I felt as I went up the ladder to the highest board, how unhappy and uncomfortable I was as I struggled to the side of the pool. Only then did I feel like I was back in control.

While I still felt safe about selling the company because I had the control of the cash, I wasn't happy or comfortable—far from it.

At the time, we were a pretty typical American couple. We had saved very little, pouring all our reserves back into the business to ensure its success. Our daughter was still a baby, so college was a long way off. My wife and I were thirty-seven and forty-one respectively, so while we thought about retirement, it wasn't pressing.

I'm an avid researcher. In fact, as Monica will tell you, she wasn't worried about what I was going to do with all that money because she knew I wasn't going to do anything stupid. I'm not a gambler, and we're alike in that we don't do what everyone else is doing. We look over the scene first and then decide which direction to take.

As that money sat in the bank, I thought about a yearly conversation I would have with my accountant. He was the tax professional, and I trusted him to make sure we weren't paying the government any more than we were required. However, as we did our yearly reckoning, our tax guy would invariably suggest Monica and I put $5,000 each into an IRA. It's a standard action many people choose as to avoid paying income taxes on a portion of that year's income, he would explain, and I would reply, "Okay, if we put $10,000 into an IRA account, how, exactly, will it save our money from taxation?"

The answer was pretty much the same every time: We were in a 28 percent federal tax bracket with another 6 percent going to the fine Commonwealth of Virginia. My accountant insisted that I would save 34 percent, or $3,400, on $10,000 in taxes if I went with an IRA contribution. Keep in mind that over and beyond our combined salaries, I was putting everything else I earned back into the sign company. Somehow, though, my accountant insisted that I still had the option of putting $10,000 into a government controlled, tax-deferred retirement account.

So I would ask him, "Okay, but why can't I take that same $10,000, write a check to the IRS for the $3,400 and put the remaining $6,600 back into the business?" Because I was in control of how much money I was making on that $6,600 investment, I thought it was a pretty good deal. So did my wife. Monica used to comment about how the accountant did everything "by the book." She knew he was good, but she also knew what I was saying made more sense, even though it wasn't "status quo" thinking.

My accountant, he couldn't track with what I was trying to tell him. He was adamant, insisting every year that my wife and I fund those IRA's, and every year I would just write the check to the IRS and put the rest of the money back into my business because I knew with certainty the following:

- Our earnings went back into the business to purchase supplies and assets to improve our company's productivity, which created more money. This allowed us to keep our money in an environment creating a reasonable rate-of-return.
- As long as the work was completed and delivered, our money would never be exposed to loss.
- We controlled the company, so we controlled the money.
- We kept our working capital account in a money market account (although knowing what I know today, I would have done it differently).
- We minimized our tax liability by managing our cash-flow and expenses through a properly managed legal entity.

When I sold my business for a half a million dollars, I was really glad I had stuck to my guns and refused to fund an IRA. Even though it is hard to quantify the actual rate of return I made on the money I invested in my company to make that $500,000, I knew I did the right thing.

Sweat equity is not easily calculated, but I know that if I had put my money in an IRA, I doubt I would have enjoyed the same consistent amount of return. My money would have been in the stock market and would have been exposed to the risks of a down market. Worse, I wouldn't have been able to access my money until I turned 59½—that was 19½ long years away.

And I knew as well as anyone that the IRS was going to take their cut when the money finally was available for my use.

I would dog my accountant with the same question: "When the time finally rolls around for us to take distributions, how, in the world, are we going to know what our future tax deductions will really be?"

He'd tell me, "not to worry about it," then would mumble something about death and taxes being part of life.

This begged another question, so I'd ask him, "What about death? What if I die prematurely? Will our taxed IRA distribution be enough for my wife and kid to live on?"

My accountant would give me a blank stare and ask, "So, what do you want to do?"

Even though I wasn't sure what I wanted to do, I knew what I *didn't* want. I didn't want my money exposed to the ups and downs of the market. I didn't want it to be locked up for a couple of decades. I wanted it earning a decent rate of interest, but I still wanted some control over it. If I put my money in an IRA or even a SEP (Simple Employee Pension) which we were eligible for, I would be putting it into the stock market, and there it would sit like a clay-duck in a shooting gallery.

I'd seen a stock market drop a time or two. I knew you could lose a ton of money during a market "correction." I didn't yet know just how often markets tend to dive, dip, and drop, and I don't know if anyone in 2000 could have predicted the severity of the crash of 2008, what precipitated the Great Recession.

My Money Philosophy

In 1995, four years before I sold my business, I went to a sales training workshop. I took it because I'm not the sales type; I'm kind of quiet actually. My wife is the outgoing firecracker and the natural sales person in the family. But I thought I could use a few tips on how to sell better so it would help the sign company. The presenter did teach me a few things about how to teach people about the product I produce, but more importantly, he also put into words how I had been thinking about money. He said, "People say money isn't everything. That's true. Money may not be everything, but it's right up there with air."

Money, or having access to money, solves a lot of problems. I'm willing to bet that 90 percent of all our problems can usually be solved by writing a check. Don't get cynical here. I know you can't purchase happiness, health, love or many things—and that 10 percent you can't buy is extremely important. What I'm talking about is where we live and sleep, where and what we eat, and what we drive. It's about where our kids go to school, what sports they play, what shoes they wear, what college they will attend. When they grow up, it's about who is paying for the weddings, and when the grandbabies come, it's about their wants and needs. You like to live a quality lifestyle and want to stay mentally and physically healthy. If you think about it, the everyday concerns of most people can be solved by having the ability to write a check.

Let's face it, having money and being able to access it is pretty darned important. We have to have water, food and air to stay alive. Money is right up there with air.

I knew that if I didn't do something to grow and protect our money, I was going to be in trouble. If I only protected it, but didn't earn anything, I would only be able to take about $15,000 a year until I was ninety-five. That would have been devastating. So of course I was going to do something with it—I just didn't know what that was … yet.

I decided to go back and look at what I knew worked. When I had my business, I was putting my money in a place I could safely control. I knew what my rate-of-return on that money would be. Taxes weren't a mystery. In other words, I could eliminate the guesswork.

That became the basis of my philosophy on money and money management. After asking thousands of people what they believe, I think I can safely say this is what most people want:

They want it in a place where it is earning a reasonable rate of return but where it's protected so they can have an income stream they can use. They need it liquid so they can access it at any time, and because they've worked hard for it, they want to have at least some control over it. It is also very comforting to at least have some idea of the future tax liabilities on it.

I have come to see these elements as three rings:

- *Growth* has to do with accumulation. Is my money experiencing competitive rates of returns?
- *Protection* is extremely important. I want my money safe from risk and market volatility.
- *Income* is about my ability to distribute cash out of my savings without restrictions. It is free from the government penalizing my social security or other retirement benefits. It has everything to do with liquidity, use, and control.

I realized that if I could find something that would give me all three, then I would have a savings vehicle that would adhere to the family financial principles represented by these three rings. But what would bring the rings together?

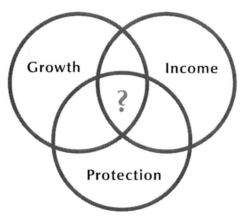

I was now on a mission. I had to find something that allowed me to *consistently* have all three rings intertwine, for my top priority was to safeguard our future earnings in a savings vehicle that would *never lose money*.

First, I looked at our home, which still had a $350,000 mortgage on it. We sat at the kitchen table one night and asked the usual question: "Why not just pay off the house and dump the pesky old monthly mortgage payment?" This is an exciting moment for most people, but as I studied it, I realized it failed the family financial principles test. The real estate market is not safe. Real estate values go up and down like those in the stock market. That mangled two of the rings right there—growth is compromised and it's not protected. While the value of the house could increase, I had no control over how much—that was entirely dependent upon the real estate market in my neighborhood. If I put three-quarters of my nest egg in my house, I wouldn't have easy access to it. That knocked off the third ring. I felt stuck: I didn't have a job, so the mortgage company wouldn't give me a home equity loan, and if I paid off that mortgage, I would lose that sweet tax deduction every year.

I decided a house is a place to live, not a place to park money. Paying off our mortgage would make it feel like our money was boxed-in by risk, tax, and inflation. No thank you.

The Financial Advisor Fiasco

So I did what most people do at that point. I met with a couple of financial advisors who recommended placing the money in a "well-balanced, managed portfolio" of stocks, bonds, and mutual funds. It sounded like some cliché out of *Money* or *Worth* magazines at the time. Something was off, so I asked, "A portfolio well-balanced by what?"

They answered with a lot of stuff about "layered-bond portfolios… off-setting mid-to-moderate risk tolerance." They wanted me to take some test to supposedly "identify my risk tolerance." I knew where that was headed. After the test supposedly "identifies" your "precise level" of your risk tolerance, they want to "scientifically design" a perfect sack of risk just for you. But it's all still risk. When the market drops, your sack risks being dumped into a river of loss with the rest. In the crash of 2008 – 2009, those who couldn't or wouldn't stay invested watched as huge sacks of retirement money were swept away.

Even though I knew that I didn't want to risk my money in any kind of market account, I thought it would be interesting to analyze the money manager's proposal for other elements. I looked closely at his annual fees. I studied the potential tax liability on our future earnings. I questioned the actual rate of return on the funds. I was hoping for something, anything, that looked reasonable.

Because I didn't know there were other choices at the time, I looked once again at the options proposed by the money managers just to see if I had missed something. Unfortunately no. Each one was subject to "open-market" activity, meaning "wide-open" to loss, even the catastrophic kind, on Wall Street.

I am so grateful today that I stood up during those meetings with the advisors, thanked them for their time, and left—as quickly as possible. If I would have listened to them, I would have been forced to wear a life vest that was ill-fitting and in the end not really safe.

After the meeting, I also realized that if I needed my money when the market was down, I would have been stuck in a dangerous state of limbo. Like I felt with my dad right behind me on the diving board, I wouldn't be able to turn back. When the market did crash, I knew that sinking feeling, like when I was in the water, going deeper than I ever wanted to. If I had a family emergency, if some dire future need meant that time would be of the essence, I would be forced to liquidate the asset at the current price, and that could be a problem. Is the stock high or low? I can't control that. If the stock is low, I'm losing the income and the potential growth, and I lose the protection factor because I'm selling the stock at a discount. In other words, all three rings are decimated.

Since I resisted placing our business profits into the house, I saved our nest egg from the real estate market collapse that precipitated the Great Recession. When those dark days in late 2008 and 2009 happened, I thought "so much for dumping our financial life-blood into their so-called well-balanced equity portfolios." Few mutual funds had come through without significant losses. So-called "layered bond" portfolios took a dive when municipalities went into default. We could have lost as much as half of our life savings in just those two years.

New Hope: A Life-Altering Discovery

I remember walking out of the meeting with the financial advisors being intensely frustrated. I felt like I had explored every popularized option at the time. I had poured over every page of every "personal finance" magazine, but they all seemed to be nothing more than a gaggle of boring geese, honking about the same-old "well-balanced portfolios" and "asset allocation," all of it tax-prone roulette, in my book.

So I went back to what I wanted: a place to protect my money from risk while letting it grow at a reasonable rate but still allowing me liquidity, and all of it growing without a major tax consequence. It shouldn't have been too much to ask but everyone in equities and real estate seemed to look at me like I'd gone stark, raving mad.

Finally, after months of research, a foray into health insurance (of all things), and exhaustive comparisons among every kind of financial strategy I could think of—*I found it.*

I discovered where I could put my money. In fact, it was *perfect.* It brought the family financial principles together in such a unique way, the rings not only overlapped, they held together no matter what you threw at it. What blew me away was that it had been there all along, backed by some of the most powerful and reliable institutions on earth.

What are You Willing to Risk?

I sincerely doubt that if you were given $450,000 as I was, or the hypothetical $1.3 million I started this chapter with, that you would want to put it in anything where you would risk losing even part of it if you knew that was all you had.

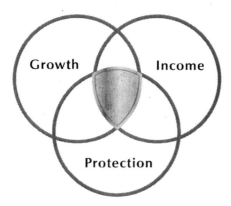

There *is* a way to keep your money safe. What I found is a shield that can truly protect the average American in times of financial crisis.

It has kept my money safe and growing at a consistent steady pace, and our accumulated cash will never, ever go away unless I decide that it does.

Right now, we are in a deceptively precarious moment in our nation's financial history. Historical trends indicate the stock market may crash again, potentially very hard. In the following pages, I'm going to share with you my discovery. As you read, know that it is your money, thus it is your choice what you want to do with it. But I hope you choose the path I did, so your money is there when you need it, like the very air that you breathe.

—PART ONE—
The Eight Major Retirement Risks
Every American Faces

There is a pretty stark reality about retirement. If we haven't saved enough and put that money in a place where it is earning a decent rate of return, we may not have enough to live on let alone handle some of the very real issues such as catastrophic illness or long-term care that happen, sometimes in our later years but sometimes not.

When we're still relatively young, say in our late thirties to forties—some of us even in our fifties—we may not think about that too much. We work. We have fun. But how many Americans, truth be told, live paycheck to paycheck? Americans, as a group, procrastinate. We don't generally budget. Many of us don't even balance our checkbooks on a regular basis. Instead of saving, we put more time, money and effort into the present concerns, like child care or, increasingly, caring for aging parents. Many of us are more concerned about where we are going on vacation or splurging on holidays than we are about saving money. We tend to forget about the things that should be our ultimate goals, things like family financial security, peace of mind, and the kind of happiness we get from having a real plan for the future.

For many of us, our retirement plan simply consists of putting some money into a 401(k), an IRA, or our home mortgage. We hope and pray that the money we put into retirement plans, and that our employers often, thankfully match, is going to hold us through our later years. If someone is nearing retirement age, this one fact probably causes more sleepless nights than anyone would like to admit.

Since many of us are facing retirement sooner or later, we scan articles on the internet. We want to know what we're up against. What we find doesn't dispel our fears. There's a lot of talk out there about baby boomers running out of money in retirement. It's a valid concern.

In order to really take control of your financial future, it is vital that you understand the eight major risks to our financial peace of mind. It's stuff Wall Street doesn't want you to know about. Brokers will tell you "don't worry about market corrections. You're in it for the long haul." What they don't realize or don't take into account is real-life events happen. From the sharp arrows of tax risk and catastrophic illness to the lethal grenades of market crashes and outliving our savings, these eight risks are being hurled at us from many directions and none of them are entirely predictable.

It is vital to understand why these eight risks are threats, so you can first confront them and then learn how to either minimize or eliminate them. If they are left unchecked, they will ruin any chance you might have for financial peace of mind.

2 The Stock Market Roller Coaster

On September 29, 2008, the U.S. banking industry collapsed. The U.S. House of Representatives rejected the president's $700 billion bank bailout plan, and the stock market reacted, as it always does in these kinds of instances, with a nose dive. I don't know how the average person reacted that day, but investors and financial institutions definitely started panicking, selling off stock at very high rates. The housing market soon followed, and Americans lost, between stocks and housing equity, around $10.2 *trillion*. The S&P, one of the main indices that measure the average stock performance of a set number of stocks, showed a whopping 38.49 percent decline for the year, and if you measured market performance between its peak on October 9, 2008 and March 2009 when it finally started to show an uptick, equity prices fell 50 percent![1] At least one observant finance writer noted that the amount of money lost that year would have paid off the entire U.S. debt.[2]

Stock brokers weren't flinging themselves out of windows (which turns out is one of the myths of the infamous market crash of 1929), but as the market kept sinking, people were faced with the fact the money being flushed away in the market wasn't "just paper." It was their hard- earned savings, much of it in 401(k)'s and other accounts set up for retirement.

The stock market is by definition speculative and volatile. The after-shocks of a hard fall reverberate for months, even years. From the crash in September 2008 through all of 2009 massive numbers of people lost their jobs as companies closed or consolidated positions, wiping out entire job descriptions, industries, and most important, careers. For those who should have been enjoying their peak earning years, job annihilation led to the last resort for many: depleting their life savings just to survive. People who should have been able to sock away critical extra savings for an impending retirement were instead laid off, terminated, or transferred due to downsizing. Many retired early, often forcibly, and either were forced to start new careers or rely more heavily than ever on Social Security.

Some of those who lost their retirement savings have taken to the road—literally—as a way to combat the after-effects of that crash. An August, 2014, *Harper's Magazine* article reported on a growing number of elderly Americans living like nomads in their RVs, crisscrossing the country in search of minimum-wage employment offered seasonally. Social workers now call them "workkampers," and they follow such websites as *Workers On Wheels* and *Workkamper News*, where itinerant jobs are posted, working in KOA camps in the summer, selling pumpkins at Halloween, and working in vast Amazon warehouses through the Christmas season. These are not poverty stricken immigrants but modern-day migrant workers, many of them retirees in the 65-and-older age category. Some of them include people who never made enough to save, but they also count among them a former university academic advisor, the one-time head of product development for McDonalds, and a State Department teaching fellow. Those and people like them worked all their lives and saved when they could. While some of these workkampers have chosen the life-style because they are adventurous and love camping, many more suffer depression, anxiety, and marital problems—typical symptoms of those living in poverty.

Harper's researchers found that workkamper numbers are "up 60 percent over a decade earlier" in part because Social Security does not provide enough to live on—most checks hovering around $400 to $500.[3] The same *Harper's* article notes a recent AARP poll that indicates only 17 percent of seniors aged fifty to sixty-five expect to avoid working in their later years. This essentially says that an alarming 83 percent of American retirees will be either working or looking for work, possibly until the day they die.

These "Oakies of the Great Recession," serve as a stark cautionary tale of the real effects of market risk. These are people who trusted that their 401(k)'s, mutual funds, and other retirement investments were going to provide them with a decent lifestyle when they stopped working. They wagered their money, either panicking and getting out at the worst possible time or suffering devastating losses. Now they drive around the country looking for seasonal work to stay alive. I'm not saying this will happen to every person who puts their retirement savings in the stock market, but the fact that it already has to some scares me.

Evaluating Risk

Risk is the reality of investing in the stock market. The more you risk the greater the rewards is the old adage that many use for various elements in their lives—from love to investing their money. Risk does work for some parts of life, but the problem with risk when you're messing with money is that it is gambling. When you gamble, your "take"—the amount you win—goes up, and it goes down. It's inevitable, and how much it is going to go up or down no one knows. The same holds true for investing in the stock market. It's also true of the bond market, but since more people are familiar with the ups and downs of the stock market, that is what I'm going to focus on.

The only way to measure market risk is to use a "look-back" process. This is simply tracking what has happened in the stock market for the past ten, fifteen, or even twenty years. So for example, from 1930 to 1944, the worst fifteen years in stock market history, you had seven years of gains and eight years of losses.

The look back process is only as good as the years you look at. Take the six years between 2009 and 2014—the longest span of time that the market has produced double-digit returns. For five out of those six years, things look pretty good. Here's the chart showing how an initial investment of $100,000 performed in those six years:

$100,000 initial investment

Year	Return %*	Account Value
2009	23.45	$123,450
2010	12.78	$139,227
2011	1.00	$140,619
2012	13.41	$159,476
2013	29.60	$206,681
2014	11.39	$230,222
6 Yr Tot	14.91%	$230,222

* These returns represent the S&P 500 price only and do not include dividends.

You're at $230,222, a $130,222 gain over where you started. This is what we all love to see. However, this doesn't show the crash of 2008 when the market dived a negative 38.49 percent.

If we look back fifteen years to 2000, which is a more accurate picture of what has happened in the stock market, this is what the S&P measured:

$100,000 initial investment

Year	Return %*	Account Value
2000	-10.14	$89,860
2001	-13.04	$78,142
2002	-23.37	$59,880
2003	26.38	$75,676
2004	8.99	$82,479
2005	3.00	$84,953
2006	13.62	$96,524
2007	3.53	$99,931
2008	-38.49	$61,468
2009	23.45	$75,882
2010	12.78	$85,580
2011	1.00	$86,436
2012	13.41	$98,027
2013	29.60	$127,043
2014	11.39	$141,513
15 Yr Tot	**2.34%**	**$141,513**

* These returns represent the S&P 500 price only and do not include dividends.

This is a far more accurate picture of what happens with the stock market. Your initial $100,000 is now showing only a $41,513 gain, but you had to endure thirteen very long years of your money dipping below that initial number. This assumes you held the investment; you didn't pull your money out or start taking distributions. The market is truly a roller coaster with some incredible highs but also some devastating lows.

Someone actually graphed the emotions that an investor experiences when their money is trading on the market:[4]

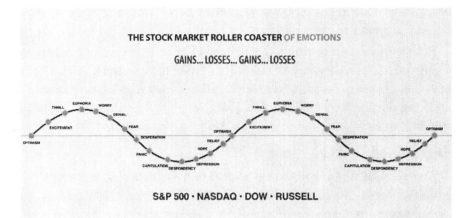

It is up and down. It's the same up-and-down emotional ride that gamblers take. Is this a roller coaster you're willing to ride, year in and year out, when you know it is your money—the stuff you expect to live on comfortably for the rest of your lives?

Adding in Market Quirks

There is an inherent problem with this look-back method, however. It does not, because it cannot, account for all the quirks of investing. For example, look back methods only measure indices. If your portfolio had stocks that performed worse than the average index, you would have lost even more money. Look backs also assume that you didn't jump out when the market tanked. For example, if you pulled your money out in 2008, your original, hypothetical $100,000 investment would have fared far worse.

There are other variables that no one can account for when it comes to trying to predict what the market is going to do. The market behaves based on what is happening in the financial world at any given moment. What happens if there is another housing boom—or bust? What happens when Russia or China, countries that hold billions of dollars of U.S. currency, decide to unload it all of a sudden?

A market look back can only be an indicator of what may happen in the future, not a prediction, because we will never have an identical situation going forward as we had in the past. You also don't know what is going to trigger a market decline or when it's going to happen, like a terrorist attack or a natural disaster, and you certainly don't know how long a recession or worse a depression is going to last.

So when you're evaluating risk, you need to know that you are, essentially, trying to look into a crystal ball that will forever remain opaque. You can't see in it. You can say to yourself, "well, I think the market is going to get better," and keep putting your money into a 401(k) or mutual funds, but every time you do, you are risking the money you have worked so diligently to earn.

How to Read Market Returns

Mark Twain was known to say there are lies, damn lies, and statistics. Statistics come last in that list because they are notoriously and easily manipulated—remember the "four out of five dentists prefer sugarless gum" in the Trident Gum ads in the 1970s? It looks like an overwhelming majority of dentists prefer you chew sugarless gum, but the statistic is a manipulation of the actual study. Many of us always wondered what the fifth dentist said (chew sugar-laden gum? I doubt it). The actual study found that four out of five dentists actually said that *if* a person is going to chew gum, they prefer that it is sugarless.[5] They weren't recommending gum at all; the statistic, however, was made to look otherwise.

Average versus Actual

Market rate of returns are another statistic that is consistently manipulated, sometimes knowingly sometimes not, by financial writers and advisors. You might hear or read that there is a 25 percent average rate of return on market investments over the course of a certain number of years. The "average" is the statistic that is manipulated.

Here is what I mean, using numbers that would never happen, but it shows you how averaging works:

Take a $100,000 investment.

Year one you double your money. You have $200,000.

Year two you lose 50 percent. You now have $100,000.

Year three it goes back up 100 percent again. You have $200,000.

Year four it goes back down 50 percent. You have $100,000.

Do the math: up 200 percent and down 100 percent over four years equals 100 percent. Divide that by four years and you get an average of 25 percent. The problem is you have not earned 25 percent annual return on your money. You do not have $200,000 in your account. You have $100,000, so the *actual* return on your money is zero percent.

The reality is an even bleaker picture. What happens if you put in $100,000 in year one but the market dips 25 percent that first year? Will you recover your money if the market recovers 25 percent the next year? Unfortunately, no. While a loss of 25 percent and a gain of 25 percent mathematically creates an *average* of zero, if you lose 25 percent of your money in one year and gain 25 percent on your money the next year, you've *actually* lost 6.25 percent of the original value of the money.

Let me show you how actual versus average played out in real time from 2007 to 2014.

In the charts below, I show the actual rates of return on the S&P 500 index from 2007 through 2014: 4.9 percent, the number you get when you calculate each year's gains and losses. Then I show the "average" return rate of 7 percent. That figure comes from adding up all the return percentages for those eight years (54.57 percent) and dividing that by eight. You get 7.08 percent. So the "average" rate of return from 2007 to 2014 is 7.08 percent.

Here are the comparisons:

S&P 500 actual rates of return: 4.90 percent.

$100,000 initial investment		
Year	S&P Return %	Account Value
2007	3.53	$103,530
2008	-38.49	$63,681
2009	23.45	$78,614
2010	12.78	$88,661
2011	1.00	$89,548
2012	13.41	$101,556
2013	29.60	$131,617
2014	11.39	$146,608
8 Yr Tot	4.90%	$146,608

The "average" rate of return of 7 percent:

$100,000 initial investment

Year	Avg Return %	Account Value
2007	7.00	$107,000
2008	7.00	$114,490
2009	7.00	$122,504
2010	7.00	$131,079
2011	7.00	$140,255
2012	7.00	$150,073
2013	7.00	$160,578
2014	7.00	$171,818
8 Yr Tot	**7.00%**	**$171,818**

The difference between the "average" and the "actual" is $25,210—pretty significant.

Math doesn't equal money. View a video on average versus actual returns at www.myfamilyfinancialmiracle.com/video.

Sequence of Return Risks

There is something even more insidious going on that you have to understand when it comes to market risk. As I showed you with the average versus actual return above, when the market drops, say, 10 percent in one year, you don't recover all your money if the market recovers 10 percent the next year. You actually need the market to perform 11.11 percent to make your money back and get to your base investment. To add to your retirement portfolio, the market would have to do better than the 11.11 percent.

If you look at the example above, you see the math play out. In year 2007, your $100,000 grew, but when it tanked in 2008, you lost over 38 percent on your entire account. Your account balance went down to $63,681. Then, even though the market did quite well the next year, 24.45 percent, you made that 24.45 percent on the ending balance of the previous year: $63,681, which gave you a total of $78,614. Yes you made money back on your loss, but you would still be down around 23 percent of your original investment.

If you are still working and putting money into the account every year, then you will recover quicker because the percentages are calculated based on the amount of money you have in at any given time.

But what happens if you have retired, and you are taking your yearly income distributions? Let's say you have decided that you want to take out 4 percent of your savings every year as your retirement income. This is the money you are living on. You are not putting any additional money into the account, so you're not building the account back up. You are depleting it year by year.

This is called poor "sequence of returns." This is what devastated so many retirement accounts in the crash of 2008. It is what actually happens when you take money out of your equity account to live on *and* the market drops in value.

For example, let's say you retired in 2007. The market showed a 3.53 percent return but you took 4 percent. That means you depleted your account a negative .47 percent. You would have an account balance of a little less than $100,000 for the year.

The market crashes in 2008. So that 38.49 percent loss would have happened on less than $100,000. But on top of that, you would have taken out your 4 percent distribution. That means your account was depleted 42.49 percent, leaving you around $57,000 on your original hundred thousand dollars. To get your money back to where you started, the market would have to perform at an unrealistic 74.76 percent the next year.

When the market tanks and you're taking distributions, the risk to your money is exponential. It is why the grade for the family financial principles test in terms of the stock market is a big, fat F.

If I could wave a magic wand in the regulatory world, I wish financial planners would be required to show consumers—you, the reader—the real impact down markets have on retirement savings.

> To see an example of poor sequence of returns, view a video at
> www.myfamilyfinancialmiracle.com/video.

I'm fifty-five. If I lost 42 percent of my retirement savings in a market crash, it would mean that I would have to stay in the work force many more years past sixty-five, the year I planned to retire. I would have to try to recover my losses by adding more dollars to my savings, and earn a higher rate of return on the money I had invested in the market originally. That's assuming the market held steady and didn't dip or downturn again. That is a roller coaster I don't think I would find enjoyable, year in and year out.

Fees and Commissions

Amusement park rides always come at a cost. Walk into any major park with your family, the kind with all the great rides, and you're immediately out a couple hundred bucks. Add food, water, and souvenirs, and you've dropped a hefty amount of cash for your day of fun. The roller coaster called the stock market is no different.

Part of the reality of investing in the stock market is that you have to pay someone to do the trading for you. You cannot, by law, buy and sell stock on the stock market unless you have a broker's license. This holds true for mutual funds, 401(k)s, IRAs, and all other retirement vehicles tied to the stock or bond market. Someone, like a fund manager or your financial advisor, is managing those accounts for you.

These brokers, fund managers, and financial advisors are making money on your money. Making money to help someone manage their money is fine—around three hundred thousand people in America earn their living this way. The question is, how much are they making?

Your stock broker or fund manager either charges your account a monthly fee to handle your money for you or makes a commission on your trading orders (to buy or sell stock) to the market. If your broker charges commissions, you are charged every time you trade, no matter if you are buying or selling a stock. It used to be brokers charged you for giving advice on which assets to pick and how to invest them. While that particular cost has gone mostly by the wayside of the internet because that's where most people do their trading, I have heard of some brokers still charging commissions. Online trading has taken the money manager out of the equation. Online trades typically charge a flat rate per trade, or small accounts have the option of paying a flat unlimited trading fee of 1/10 of 1 percent on the account value.

Fees can eat up the gains you make in the market. Here is a realistic picture of what happens based on an equity account with a 28 percent tax and .75 percent management fee:

Equity Account Charges and Expense Detail*

Deposit	Avg Ret	Act Gains	Inc Tax	Mgmt Fee	Total
$12,000	31.57%	$3,760	-$175	-$90	-$265
$12,000	18.56%	$5,108	-$301	-$245	-$546
$12,000	5.10%	$2,248	-$375	-$348	-$723
$12,000	16.61%	$9,569	-$673	-$504	-$1,177
$12,000	31.69%	$24,720	-$960	-$770	-$1,730
$12,000	-3.10%	-$3,503	-$1,087	-$821	-$1,908
$12,000	30.47%	$36,437	-$1,383	-$1,170	-$2,553
$12,000	7.62%	$12,609	-$1,452	-$1,336	-$2,788
$12,000	10.08%	$18,879	-$1,571	-$1,546	-$3,117
$12,000	1.32%	$2,839	-$1,709	-$1,634	-$3,343
			-$9,686	-$8,464	-$18,150

*These returns include dividends, and dividends are taxed.

Each year you're putting in the same amount. You can see the up and down action of your rate of return for each year with the dollar amount you made on that money every year. But notice that even when the market loses money, you are still paying a management fee and income tax. So by the end of ten years, the total amount you've paid for fees and commissions is substantial.

With the illustration you can see the money you make—or lose—in any given year is reduced by the amount of money your broker or fund manager is charging.

Conflict of Interest

This fee business gets even worse. In February 2015, the Executive Office of the President of the United States issued a report on "The Effects of Conflicted Investment Advice on Retirement Savings."[6] While not the most exciting title, the contents of the report make any person investing in the stock or bond markets take notice. On page one, the report says:

Selecting and managing IRA investments can be a challenging and time-consuming task, frequently one of the most complex financial decisions in a person's life, and many Americans turn to professional advisers for assistance. However, financial advisers are often compensated through fees and commissions that depend on their clients' actions. Such fee structures generate acute conflicts of interest: *the best recommendation for the saver may not be the best recommendation for the adviser's bottom line* (italics mine).

Let's pull this long quote apart. First, while it says "IRA investments" you could insert any kind of investment from 401(k), to 529 plans for college savings, to mutual funds, to direct trading on the market. Investing is challenging and time-consuming precisely because it is "one of the most complex financial decisions in a person's life." In other words, most people are not educated well enough to really know what they're doing on the stock market. It is a brutal job—think of the pictures and movies you've seen about stock brokers. They are a rather stressed out bunch of people.

When you're not educated about how something as complex as the stock market works, you definitely are risking your money simply because you can make extremely costly mistakes: you could pull your money before you should, make a really bad trade, or leave your money in too long. The variations on the theme of "bad trading" are endless. To complicate matters, if you are confused over all the complex pricing that comes with financial advice, you risk losing even more.

So you rely on financial advisers to help you, but oftentimes they represent the "acute conflict of interest" noted above. The report defines conflicted advice as "payments to the adviser that depend on the actions taken by the advisee," which means that "the advice that is best for [the adviser's] own bottom line may not be the advice that is best for their customer's savings" (6). When a broker or fund manager makes money every time you trade, they risk giving you advice that is going to help their bottom line, not yours. Even though many financial advisers hold themselves to high standards and take their fiduciary responsibility to you and your money very seriously, it is human nature to make decisions that are going to benefit yourself as well as, or over, others.

Even if your advisor is honestly trying to take care of you, the report found the research comparing mutual funds sold directly to savers or sold through "intermediaries" like advisors didn't look good: "funds characterized by conflicted payments significantly underperform funds sold directly to savers" because "conflicted intermediaries"—the advisors—"significantly increased annual fees, significantly decreased annual after-fee returns, and slightly increased risk-taking relative to the [default investment option]"(11). What all that means is advisors are going to charge you more to manage your money; they will keep you in the market longer, keeping you fully invested instead of pulling it out and moving it into cash or a stable value fund. Remember, they make an annual fee on the cash value of the fund regardless if it made money or not.

The Myth of Buy and Hold

Why, you might ask, is the Executive Office of the President concerned about whether or not your broker or financial adviser is acting in your best interest? I'll get to that answer in the next chapter. For now, just know that the money you make when you have any investments in the stock market, including employer-matched funds in a 401(k), is not safe. The stock market, while it can make you fantastic gains, also leaves your money, and thus you, very vulnerable.

I don't ever want to lie in bed at night wondering if I'm going to have enough, if I'm going to get out in time, if there is a way to stop the losses that are inevitable. I don't know about you, but I don't want to spend even a minute of my life worrying about whether or not I'm going to lose my retirement money. It's like worrying about whether my car is going to start or not.

If I have a good battery, it's going to start every time. If my battery is old and running out of power, then I worry how I'm going to get from point A to point B. We all know that horrible feeling when we try starting our car, but instead of turning over with a nice *vroom*, it goes *wroo, wroo, wroo*. Finally it starts, but then you spend your whole trip wondering if it's going to start again once you turn it off.

The simple fix to the battery problem is to go down to the automotive store and fork over $90 for a new one. Most of the time, the nice clerks will even install it for you. However, how many people do you know who will not spend the $90 to get a new battery? They'll spend all their time worrying about whether their car is going to start, and when their battery finally gives out, they're stuck with at least a $100 tow bill *and* the $90 for the battery.

This is what people do with their money. When the market dips, they think, all I need to do is just wait a little bit longer. They even make themselves sick over it, but they listen to their broker who tells them: "buy and hold," which means "don't panic. Don't dump your investment, just ride it out." So they leave their money where it's not safe; they pray they'll make a little bit more. They get their hopes up because they see the market going up and up. But all of a sudden the market tanks. They think, "I should have gotten out," but they just lost 10 percent, 22 percent, or God forbid 38 percent of their money. It's gone. The only time someone can wave a magic wand and "poof" it all comes back is if they win the lottery or they get a nice tidy inheritance from their parents or some long-lost uncle.

There are some who love playing the market. There are those who believe that past performance does guarantee future results. But wouldn't it be nice if you didn't have to worry about the roller coaster, even one bit?

I'm not that much of a gamblin' man, to be honest. I would rather have my money in a place that is guaranteed, by contract, not to lose money in any market downturn. For when you risk your retirement, you're risking your future. Are you really willing to do that? I've found that there is just as much money to be made in not messing with the losing opportunity as there is in picking the apparent winners.

3 Taxes and the Money Bubble

What is it about taxes that people just don't like? When our tax money supports our roads and bridges, our schools and our military, we're pretty much okay with that. When our hard-earned money goes to support an over-bloated bureaucracy, we get more than a little upset about having to pay more taxes to finance all of it. I think it's safe to say that people do not like paying higher taxes and are always for paying lower taxes.

Because taxes are part of the government, discussing them is always going to bump up against the political. Retirement affects all Americans, no matter how you vote on election day, and to state the issue of taxes in broad terms, politicians either support higher taxes—especially for those in the upper-income levels of society—or argue that we should cut spending to address the gargantuan budget deficits we have created with social spending (including healthcare) and over-the-top bailouts.

In February 2015, President Barak Obama submitted his budget proposal to Congress. It was all over the internet from CNBC to WND (WorldNetDaily). According to all accounts, it contained over a dozen provisions targeting qualified retirement accounts—the tax postponed kind like your 401(k), IRAs and even ROTHS. *MarketWatch*, a subsidiary of the Dow Jones, reported the news but was also very clear about the fact that the president's budget is "really more of a 'wish list' than anything else, but it's a good indication of where the administration is headed."[7] In other words, while it hasn't happened yet, at least one branch of the government has overt designs on some or all of your retirement savings, depending on where you have your money stashed.

As of 2013 there was 20.8 trillion dollars sitting in retirement accounts.[8] A pretty large chunk of that money hasn't been taxed yet because you don't have to pay taxes on it until you take the money out—and that's what prompts the government to constantly want to change the tax codes. They want their share. They actually take their share consistently every year as more and more people retire, yet many people don't understand the extent to which their savings is going to be taxed.

Whatever the side of the political spectrum you sit on, the fact remains, taxes are a fact of life, and if the stock market presents an overt risk to your money, taxes are the insidious, hidden threat that can eat away at your retirement savings much like the way termites slowly, consistently devour an old wooden home.

The Money Bubble

We think we pay a lot of taxes now; our highest tax bracket is 39.60 percent. That is nothing compared to where it was in 1944 when it peaked at 94 percent for the highest wage earners then held at a steady 90 percent through the 1950s.[9] David M. Walker, the Comptroller General of the U.S. and the head of the Government Accountability Office (basically the head CPA of the US and our nation's chief auditor), from 1998 to 2009, has travelled the country telling Americans that given our current fiscal path of very high spending, our government is going to have to double our taxes or we're going to go bankrupt.[10]

I'm in that highest tax bracket, and the idea of paying 80 percent of my income to the government just makes me plain mad because I know what I'm paying for. It's called the money bubble.

When we think of bubbles, we like to think of the nice kind, like our kids or grandkids blowing bubbles or the set of the Lawrence Welk show if you can remember that far back. But there are also bad bubbles like blisters or pimples—the kind that hurt when you pop them.

Remember the dot.com bubble of the late 1990s or the housing bubble of the mid 2000s? We're already familiar with over-blown bubbles: when you ride them, they produce fantastic amounts of cash, but when they burst—and they always do—we lose far too much for comfort.

There is a very big, very bad, and potentially very painful bubble called the money bubble that is growing by the hour thanks to the great bubble machine in Washington called the Federal Reserve—"the Fed" for short.

The Fed feeds this money bubble full of debt, debt so large that it is truly unfathomable to most of us.

We have a national life style of debt. If someone said they're debt free, you would think they were an alien. But the amount of debt that hangs precariously over our heads is mostly made up of government entitlements.

To understand the money bubble, you first have to grasp the concept of one trillion. If you were to guess what year it was one trillion seconds ago, what would be your answer? We keep hearing that it's a pretty big number, so maybe you'd guess 1066, the year the French Duke, William the Conqueror, took over England.

That's not even close. Try 30,000 B.C. If you made seconds into dollars, it would take you 32,015 years to spend $1 trillion.[11] That would be enough dollar bills stacked on top of each other to go *past* the moon.

> To view a demonstration of the size of $1 trillion,
> please visit www.myfamilyfinancialmiracle.com/video.

Keep that concept firmly in your mind so that the enormity of this bubble will make sense.

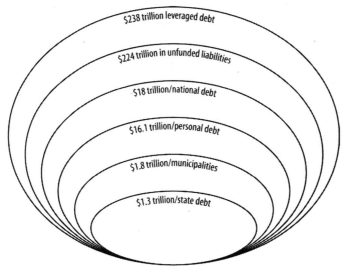

$238 trillion leveraged debt

$224 trillion in unfunded liabilities

$18 trillion/national debt

$16.1 trillion/personal debt

$1.8 trillion/municipalities

$1.3 trillion/state debt

$500 trillion total debt

The money bubble can be illustrated as a set of concentric circles. Inside the inner circle of the U.S. debt-fueled money bubble is of course the national debt. Right now that stands at about $18 trillion. (If you spent a dollar a day, you'd have to go back to *early* prehistoric times to spend that much.)

The debt for all the states in the US equals about $1.3 trillion. This is why state employee pensions are running out of money.

Next comes local municipalities. They owe about $1.8 trillion, and many of them are teetering on the edge of bankruptcy.

Now what balloons this out to something that is over-the-top scary is the US's total of unfunded liabilities like Medicare and Social Security. It stands at $224 trillion. Add to that all our leveraged debt from the derivatives market (think oil futures and stuff like that), you're looking at $235 trillion more.

Student loan debt is at $1.3 trillion, credit cards make up a mere $900 billion, and we debt hungry Americans hold about $16.1 trillion in personal debt.

Add that up, and the US money bubble of debt is close to *five hundred trillion* dollars. I don't know if anyone can really fathom how much money that really is.

I have already noted that anything can tip the market into a decline. Add to terrorism and bank meltdowns such things as political upheaval, especially when there are economic consequences, impact from climate change such as hurricanes and tsunamis, and cyberterrorism, and you have some very sharp needles that will burst the debt bubble in a heartbeat.

Unfortunately we cannot borrow, spend, or even print our way out of it with ever-increasing mountains of something called fiat money (money that derives its value from government regulation or law as opposed to being based on something like gold or silver). It really is getting worse by the second—just go to USDebtclock.org and watch the national debt rise by about a hundred thousand dollars in less than a minute (there is interest on all the debt, and when you're talking trillions, it adds up pretty darn fast.)

However, the government can try to tax its way out of it, and that's why your not-yet-taxed 401(k)s and IRAs are so appealing to the government.

Tax Buckets

Where are these taxes coming from? Over the years, I have come to realize that there are misconceptions about various definitions and concepts having to do with taxes. So, in order to help you educate yourself, I'm going to go over some of the basics.

Our income is taxed. We all know that. The government, right now, does not double tax your income. If you pay income tax on what you've earned and then put some of that already-taxed money into a savings account, it's called "after tax money," and the government is only going to tax the interest you make in that savings account, not the principal.

These are ***annual tax accounts.*** They require that you pay taxes on the account's growth every year. This generally holds for money in CD's and money market accounts as well as money you make in mutual funds, stocks, and bonds. The amount of tax you pay on this interest is going to vary depending on what kind of investment vehicle you have your money in. If you're making money in stocks, you're often paid on dividends, and you pay up to a 20 percent capital gains tax. It is important to note that the capital gains tax is no longer one flat rate. It varies depending upon your income; it also includes additional capital gains rates and if you're in the top income strata of investors, you are also taxed 3.8 percent for Medicare.[12] If you have your money in a CD, and it's not attached to any kind of tax-deferred account, then you pay the tax noted on the 1099 your bank is going to send you. Tax codes are notoriously complicated: the IRS tax codes and regulations make up around seventy thousand pages.[13] I'm not a CPA or a tax lawyer, so you want to consult with them about what kind of tax you pay and how much. The point is, you pay taxes every year on that money, and the amount you pay is always at the whim of the government.

If you have large amounts of money in annual tax accounts, the taxes you pay on the interest you're earning in those accounts can add up quickly. For example, let's say you put $100,000 after tax dollars into a mutual fund, and you make 5 percent on your investment. You're taxed on the $5,000 you make. If you're taxed 30 percent total (both federal and state) on the interest, your "take home" on that $5,000 is $3,500. Fifteen hundred bucks is a chunk, no matter how wealthy you are. It gets even worse when you consider that the money you have in most of these taxable accounts is compounding, which means you're making money on the money you've earned in interest. I could chart it out, but the simplicity is, the more money you make the more tax you pay. The higher the tax rate, the more you're going to pay, and it doesn't take much to get hit with a fairly high tax bill on these types of accounts.

Tax-postponed accounts (often referred to as tax-deferred) are the other taxable entities. I prefer "postponed" over "deferred" because it makes more real the inevitability of taxes being levied against the dollars you earn. Tax-postponed may have some advantages in the short term, but we all know Uncle Sam wants his share of the money we earn. You take the risk, but Uncle Sam gets to share in the reward.

Tax-postponed plans are all the "qualified plans" employers and employees use now for retirement. They were created when the traditional "defined benefit" pension plans were replaced with "defined contribution" plans that we have in effect today.

The "defined benefit" pensions were the kind that our parents retired on, where the employer had all the responsibility for making sure the money they had in their pension account was invested well and growing at a decent amount so that the paychecks for their retired, loyal workers who had stayed with them for thirty plus years would be covered.

Pensions in the private sector started going by the wayside in the early 1980s when the steel and airlines industries went belly up, and it was discovered that their pension plans had been sucked dry. In other words they had "unfunded liabilities," and the money they were on the hook for, for all their retirees, wasn't there. (If this sounds like what you've heard about Social Security, you're correct. We'll get to that hornet's nest in a minute.)

There were other issues: the government, worried that they would have a lot of really poor retirees, regulated pensions. While on the one hand this is a good thing because Americans need to put something away for retirement, government regulations always cost more money than they're supposed to. Add to that the fact that workers were living longer, so pension funds in all sectors were quickly running out of money. This is an enormous issue today with pension funds for public employees: teachers, post office workers, military personnel, and the millions of bureaucrats who worked at all levels of government from the local Department of Motor Vehicles to the CPAs who worked in the US Government Accountability Office, the office that's supposed to tell us things like how much the Affordable Care Act, otherwise known as Obamacare, is costing us. The media is full of news about bankrupt state and local pensions, news that translates into people not getting their retirement checks every month.[14]

Out of the ashes of under-funded pension plans came the 401(k), which is actually named for the tax code that regulates it. It is the most well-known of the "defined contribution" plans, where employers contribute to the plan with pre-tax dollars. It solved a huge problem for employers and employees alike. Employers were no longer on the hook for managing pension funds and they got to write off their contribution to the employee's account. A more mobile work force could take their retirement with them from job to job. The difference between the old pension plan and the new 401(k) was who was responsible for the retirement investments. It now lay with the employee. Everything looked great through the 1980s and 1990s until the first major market bubble—the dot.com boom—burst.[15] But qualified plans were here to stay, and we have been dealing with the consequences ever since.

There are actually four phases our retirement money goes through: accumulation, where we are building the account; distribution, where we are taking money out to live on in retirement; the wealth preservation, which coincides with distribution because you want to preserve your wealth while you are still living a decent lifestyle; and finally the wealth transfer or legacy phase, where the money you have worked so diligently to manage is now being transferred to your heirs.

The 401 (k) and other qualified plans are what most people rely on for their retirement. Your pre-tax money is going into an investment vehicle, but you don't pay taxes on it today, so your tax bill is lower. Your money is in an account hopefully growing, earning interest and/or dividends. You're told you won't have as big a tax hit when you take the money out in the distribution phase because you won't be making as much hence you won't be taxed as much.

There is something important about 401(k)s that I have to mention. A lot of people bash them. I'm not a big fan of them myself because of the alternative I found, but many miss this crucial fact. If it weren't for 401(k)s and Social Security, many Americans wouldn't save a cent. They are both forced saver's plans. A T.V. anchorwoman in Denver said it best. While she's working, she'll continue to put the same amount of money into a 401(k) that her employer matches. It's the matching funds that she likes, but she also knows the inevitable is going to happen. When you take your distributions from your qualified plans, you will pay taxes. More than you were prepared for in many cases.

The Tax Hits

Let's examine the prevailing idea that you won't pay as much in taxes when you retire as you would when you're working. That may be true now, but will it remain true in the future? We are still at historically low tax-rate levels, and we are going to have to handle that money bubble at some point. As one finance guy put it, "low tax rates and big deficits are a toxic combination."[16] Most all the financial pundits agree that taxes are going to have to be raised to handle at least some of the mountain of debt we face.

Okay, but let's still assume that tax rates are going to stay the same for the next ten to twenty years. The first year you retire, you start taking distributions, and that's when reality hits. If your once tax-deferred money is coming from your investments in the stock market, you will now be responsible to pay the prevailing income tax on those distributions. If you have money in CD's and money markets, you have to continue to handle the 1099 taxes on the money you make from those.

However, the biggest tax problem in retirement is with deductions—or the lack thereof.

I've lost count of the number of retired people who come to me and complain that they are paying as much or more in taxes. So I ask them, "what are your deductions?"

The inevitable answer, "deductions? What deductions?!"

While tax hikes are hypothetical, lost deductions are very real. There are four major deductions most Americans take in their wage earning years that are lost in retirement:

Mortgage interest—remember in chapter 1 when I decided not to pay off my house? I didn't want to lose the deduction of the interest on my mortgage. But at some point, your house is going to be paid off, and that usually happens just before or around retirement, and so you don't get to deduct the interest any more.

Your children—when you retire, you're kids are probably grown and hopefully out of the house. If they aren't, they are too old to be declared a dependent. So you lose both the exemption (a monetary sum that reduces your taxable income) and the tax credit (the amount of money you can offset against the tax liability—your tax bill.)

You no longer make your retirement plan contributions—you're now taking it as income, thus you lost that deduction. Most retirees also no longer contribute monetarily to charities because they are on a fixed income, and even if they contribute their time, that doesn't count as a tax deduction.

What do you have left? Not much, so often the government is taking more tax dollars even though you're taxable income is less than it was when you were working.

The Ticking Time Bomb

Social Security, the money the government promised to pay us when we're retired, has also become a tax liability. It wasn't supposed to be this way. When it was first framed by FDR's administration as part of the "New Deal" with America, it was set up as a trust account. Your employer took money out of your paycheck every month and sent it to the Social Security administration. It was specifically an interest-earning fund from which the employee could withdraw a set amount of money in their later years. As I said above, it's a forced saver's plan. In fact, it's the most successful government-run program in U.S. history.

The problem came about because congress saw this massive amount of money sitting in a trust. They started using it and writing giant IOUs, but never really figured out a way to make good on those notes.

We have been hearing for years about how the Social Security administration is either bankrupt or close to it. Part of the issues is that when the law was first enacted, there were forty-two working people contributing into the fund for every one person taking money out. Sixty-five was the age you were supposed to retire and take Social Security payments, but people weren't living that long. Sixty-two was the average life-expectancy.

Right now, there are three people contributing to the fund to every one person taking Social Security, and with Baby Boomers retiring in droves, the ratio is going to quickly reduce down to two to one.[17] That's a huge difference, and when you factor in that 1) people are living far longer than sixty-two (by twenty to thirty years!), and 2) since the government has been dipping into the account for years but not paying back the IOUs, there is no money in the Social Security trust fund earning interest.

Just to give you an idea of how big a problem this is, in 2012, 76 percent of every tax dollar went to pay for Social Security and Medicare. It's far more now that the Affordable Care Act (a.k.a. Obamacare) is in full swing. It could balloon to 92 cents of every tax dollar by the year 2020.[18] That leaves nothing for the hundreds of government programs, from all the welfare programs to the US Forest Service, the Centers for Disease Control, the Peace Corps, the State Department, and the Army, Navy, Air Force, and Marines. I think you get the picture.

Remember, there's supposed to be over $200 trillion in the Social Security trust earning interest. Instead, it's an "unfunded liability," meaning that there isn't any money set aside.

I've seen comparisons between Social Security and Ponzi schemes. Ponzi schemes, Bernie Madoff reminded us all-too-painfully well, is when the person operating the fund, like Madoff, pays returns to its investors from new money brought in by new investors, rather than from the profit earned by the operator. It's illegal for everyone except the Social Security Administration apparently.

How does the government solve problems like this it creates? It either prints more money or it raises taxes. (We wish it would also cut spending, and while that would be the most fiscally responsible thing to do, I'm not holding my breath). Back in 1983, President Ronald Regan and House Speaker Tip O'Neill decided that in order to keep Social Security afloat, the government needed to tax that benefit. It hadn't been taxed before. It was income you had earned, they figured, so now up to 50 percent of your Social Security can be taxed if you and your spouse's combined income is between $32,000 and $44,000 a year. President Bill Clinton upped the tax to 85 percent if you and your spouse claim more than $44,000 a year.[19] While this was not at all what FDR had in mind, the tax is here to stay. This is how it works: Let's say your retirement distributions from all your retirement accounts comes to $34,000 a year, $2833.33 per month. Part of that is your Social Security check, which is $900 a month. So you're going to have to pay income tax on 50 percent of the $900 per month social security benefit, or income taxes on $450. At a 25 percent federal income tax rate your tax on the $900 benefit would be $112.50. Couple that with the taxes you will have to pay on the remaining $1,933, and your monthly income dwindles down even more.

Social Security income isn't much. Very few people I know can actually live off their Social Security checks. But $32,000 a year in today's economy isn't that much money either, and the additional $112.50 per month would be a blessing for many. In my opinion, the government has been fiscally irresponsible for many, many years, you're now going to be taxed on part of your Social Security benefit by the government who wasn't taking care of the money—your money—in the first place.

It becomes an elaborate puzzle for many retirees, figuring out how much money they can take from their IRAs and other investments without compromising their Social Security check.

As many people know, when you turn 70 ½ you *must* by law withdraw a certain amount from your IRAs—the account in which most of the qualified monies end up. They're called RMDs—required minimum distributions. You can start taking withdrawals at 59 ½, and the government likes that. They can start collecting their tax. However, RMDs are calculated by law, and if you don't take it when you're supposed to, you're *fined* 50 percent of the RMD for that year. It's called an "excise tax" but make no mistake, it's a fine. If you have any additional income from a job or rental property or municipal bonds, that figures into the whole equation. So what do you do? If you take too little from your IRA or 401(k) so you're Social Security isn't taxed, you're fined. If you take the required minimum distribution amount, then you risk having your Social Security taxed.

The government wants to take as much of our money as it can. It feels justified because every nine seconds another person retires. That means that every nine seconds, someone is applying for entitlements like Social Security. Who is going to pay for that? We are. Likely in the form of higher taxes.

If you're starting to feel like you're getting backed into a corner with all this, I understand. The solution I found is real and can shield you from even the seemingly inevitable risk of taxes. I, fortunately, am not going to get hit with the taxes I've just talked about. But in order to appreciate how much of a miracle that is, it is important to know that you're up against more than market risk and taxes. There's one more chapter of doom and gloom, and then we'll get to the good stuff. I promise.

4 The Other Six Major Risks

I had a couple in their sixties come to my office for some financial advice in the spring of 2004, a referral from one of my clients. He was a custom home builder, and his wife did all his accounting and scheduling. Their business had done well over the last twenty years, and they had accumulated enough money to retire. They had their savings in multiple places and looked like most American's retirement portfolio: 20 percent was in CD's and money market accounts. He had roughly 50 percent in a mutual fund portfolio. The other 30 percent of their funds were in his business checking account.

I asked them my usual questions: what were their plans for the future? How long did they plan on building houses, and when were they planning on retiring? They had enough savings to live comfortably, but the idea of not working on something did not sit well with the builder. He said he had to be doing something all the time to keep his mind busy. I suggested picking up a hobby he enjoyed. His immediate response was he enjoyed building stuff. "That's wonderful," I said and asked him if he had any projects in mind.

Their son was at this meeting, but he sat quietly through most of it until we started talking about future projects. He had graduated from Virginia Tech with a degree in business, and his parents, the builder and his wife, wanted to help him get started in business instead of him going to work for someone else. I could applaud that; I had done the same for myself.

I asked him how he felt about going into the residential building business like his dad. He stood up and presented a business plan he was working on to build townhouses in Virginia Beach.

I built a successful sign company that worked with a lot of local builders for many years; I had the opportunity to listen to their stories, year in and year out, about the building booms and the busts in Virginia Beach. It's definitely a feast or famine in my city for this type of business.

I loved the young man's enthusiasm, but his lack of real life experience was very concerning to me. What was more concerning was his mom and dad's overwhelming confidence in this young man's ability to be successful using their life savings. They believed in their son and his plan and were convinced that their current capital would triple from the project. I helped them as best I could and sent them on their way. I didn't hear from them for three years. In the spring of 2008, I got a phone call from the builder to set up a meeting with me. I could hear the anxiety in his voice. When we met, they were very distraught. The project they committed to as a family had failed.

From the beginning there were cost overruns. From zoning and lot preparation to construction material, everything in the original plan was costing double and taking twice as long to complete. This happened because there was a building boom, and is the case in all building booms, costs increase. The family quickly got into a cash flow problem and started using everything they saved for retirement to keep the project going.

To make things worse, there was a crash looming. It was 2008, so by the end of the year, the 50 percent of the funds that had been put in mutual funds had lost about half of its account value in the market correction. It was a perfect storm of catastrophic loss, and it was being handled by their son who had not experienced or anticipated any of these issues or challenges.

The project did get completed, but it was so far over budget that it couldn't compete on the open market, for as we all know, the 2008 market correction was precipitated by the housing bubble exploding. The properties couldn't be sold for the price needed to recover the cost, and this very nice couple lost their entire life savings when the bank took the property. Around the same time, the dad suffered a mild heart attack and was diagnosed with adult onset-diabetes. I was devastated for them.

When I say that your retirement savings—your future—is very much at risk from simply the various events and emergencies that invariably happen in life, I mean it. I have seen unbelievable things happen to people, and if we are unprepared and uneducated about what we're up against as well as being aware of alternatives to handle the problem, it can mean the difference between living comfortably for the remainder of our lives or living on barely nothing.

Life Happens

So far I've covered two of the eight major life risks: market risk and tax risk. There are five more major categories of what I call "life risks" that threaten your money:

- catastrophic illness with long-term care
- job or career risks
- legal risks
- longevity, and
- premature death risks.

We will experience more than one of these "life risks" at some point, and there is the very real possibility that all but one could happen when we're twenty-eight or forty. In other words, these are not risks only seniors face. For example, we all know someone with cancer or heart disease if we do not ourselves suffer from those maladies. We will also change careers at least once in our lives. The chances of us getting sued at some point are very high with upwards of seventy thousand lawsuits filed every day in U.S. courts. Because many of us think "oh, that won't happen to me," I am going to run through the six to help you understand that any one of them can—and will—happen.

Risk #3 Catastrophic illness with long-term care: When you're hit with catastrophic illness—the kind of illness that requires a prolonged hospital stay or recovery—you are faced with high medical bills. If you contract cancer, you have extremely high pharmaceutical bills coupled with hospital bills for surgery if that is the treatment you elect. If you have a heart attack, your hospital bill is high. In New York and Hawaii, you'll pay upwards of $100,000 a month for catastrophic care. Other areas of the country are not so expensive but still devastating at $4,000 to $12,000 month. If you have health insurance, it will cover some of the bills, but only for the health-related expenses, and usually only for so much. But that doesn't account for the lost time from work. How long can you write checks to cover the rest?

Most people think that they are invincible but unfortunately, these kinds of illnesses can strike at any time and at any age—just read Tim Lusher's blog, "The truth about recovering from a brain injury." Here's a thirty-something who suffered a potentially lethal brain infection. He obviously lived to tell about it, but his stories of other thirty-somethings who suffered catastrophic brain injuries or illnesses are eye opening. [20] Some of them will never fully recover. From brain tumors to comas, you never know—and it doesn't matter if you're twenty-five or ninety. You go to the doctor for a routine physical and you walk out of there with a diagnosis that will change your life. I know of a man who was in his thirties. He was diagnosed with a heart condition. He had a stent put in his heart—a fairly routine procedure these days, but he developed an infection during surgery and was bedridden for a year and a half. In that time, he wasn't able to work. With no income, he had to rely on the little savings he had.

With catastrophic illness comes long-term care. Long-term care isn't just an issue for seniors. It doesn't matter how old you are, if you're in an accident or suffer a debilitating illness, you will need someone to help take care of you. That help can be costly.

The costs for in-home care, assisted living, and skilled nursing care are soaring. In 2013, the average cost of a one-year stay in a private care facility topped over $90,000. According to one study, the cost of long-term care is projected to double in the next fifteen years. Home health care and assisted living, which cost on average around $40,000 in 2013, is projected to rise to around $60,000 to $65,000 by 2028. Can your retirement savings cover that?

While many of us are aware of this potential drain on our savings, what many of us don't know is only twenty-four insurance companies cover long-term care. Such giants as MetLife, Prudential, and Unum Group, have withdrawn their long-term care coverage from the market, some as far back as 2009. This is concerning considering one out of five thousand people have a chance of getting in a car accident. One out of twelve thousand people will suffer the devastation of a house fire. Three out of seven people will need catastrophic long-term care at some point in their lives. It is a potentially terrible drain on your finances.

Risk #4 Job loss or job interrupted is another of the "life happens" moments that can pose a major risk to your retirement savings. It is a fact of life that workers get laid off, terminated, or transferred and are forced to start new careers. Losing your job is never easy, but it's become down-right problematic in recent years. In 2009, while the world was reeling from the devastating market corrections in late 2008, twenty thousand people were losing their jobs every day. In 2013, a Post Miller Center poll found that six out of ten workers worried that they would lose their job, and 65 percent of those polled said they worried about whether their family income would be enough to cover their needs. At that point in time, the US unemployment rate hovered around 7 percent with nearly three workers for every job opening.

Three out of four workers are living paycheck to paycheck, and about the same percentage (75 percent!) say they have less than six months of savings put away.[21] This study came at a time when the stock market was gaining double digits, but it still feels like the aftershocks of the Great Recession are still rumbling. What all this really means: a large percentage of the American workforce is woefully unprepared to handle retirement with any kind of ease and financial peace of mind is quickly compromised when the job is gone.

A National Poverty Center study published in March of 2013, "The Effects of the Great Recession on the Retirement Security of older Workers," corroborated the Post Miller Center poll. First, it notes that "The retirement income landscape is changing dramatically. Retirement needs are increasing as longer life expectancy has lengthened the retirement period." As most everyone will tell you, we're living longer and so we need more income to support us through the long haul, but fewer and fewer of us are saving the kind of money we need to see us through.

What the National Poverty Center found that is important here is that more workers in their late careers—fifty and older—experienced job loss than in previous recessions and it is taking them longer to find new jobs than in other times of economic downturn. Those who do find jobs often take a pay cut which makes for more instability in their lives which generally increases health risks. It's a tough situation to be in, and it's made worse because safe fixed accounts like money markets and CD's are crediting interest rate that are very low on life savings.

Risk #5 Legal risks are always present. Again, many people think "that's not going to happen to me" because they're not in a profession that has high legal risk like doctors. But with the divorce rate hovering at around 50 percent, it means that if you're married you have a 50/50 chance of being sued by your spouse to end your marriage. What about getting sued by your neighbor because they think your dog is barking too loudly? (You can do that in small claims court.) Lawsuits are expensive. They can also wreck long friendships, but people are advised by their attorneys to ask for huge amounts of "pain and suffering" damages anyway because they know insurance companies will often settle.

I was shocked when I learned the following story: a woman in her forties has an eight-year old daughter. She was driving her daughter and her daughter's best friend, also eight, to a restaurant. The two mothers of the girls were also long-time close friends. The woman who was driving had to slam on her brakes abruptly at an intersection. The daughter's best friend bumped her nose on the backrest. There was no accident, no severe situation. When she got home, the girl complained her nose hurt so her mother took her to the doctor's. There was nothing wrong. Nothing broken—no damage or problem of any kind. The mother sued her friend, the driver, for $300,000, claiming her daughter suffered trauma and psychological problems because of the slammed brakes. The mother (the person suing) called her friend of twenty years (the person driving), to talk about the lawsuit. The one told the other there was no problem, but "Please, just let the insurance company write the check." They needed the money.

Watch any station on TV and within thirty minutes, you're going to see an advertisement for some lawsuit ranging from pharmaceuticals to asbestos. A lawsuit is filed every thirty seconds and it gets worse every year. How can you shield yourself from that?

Risk #6 Longevity is the nine-hundred pound gorilla that sits in every retiree's living-room. While this only affects older seniors, it is still a major concern. I rarely have someone come into my office and declare they are going to be dead at seventy. We all want to live as long as we can, and thanks to modern medicine, we are. The *Economist* noted that over the past fifty years, "every forecast of how long people will live has fallen short."[22] The risk is that we *are* living longer than expected. Despite conjecture that such things as obesity and global warming would reverse the trend, the same article notes that people in rich countries, like us, have added 2.5 years to our lives every decade. Our grandchildren and cruise companies love that. But what is it costing? Adding an extra year to our average lifespan costs the global pension bill upwards of around $1 trillion a year according to the International Monetary Fund. (What is it with that trillion dollar mark?).[23]

What does this mean for individual Americans? Our retirement nest egg may not last us. It's the reason why reverse mortgages are so popular right now. You have equity in your home; you need funds, the bank is willing to loan you money on your home. Reverse mortgages aren't ideal; the bank isn't buying your home back from you as many believe. Rather, they are loans that must be paid back when the home is sold. The interest rates on reverse mortgages are higher than typical home equity loans, and you have to pay all the fees and such to make the loan happen.[24] This potentially leaves nothing for your heirs.

Outliving our retirement puts a tremendous burden on our relatives, especially our children. I know many children who put their plans on hold because they have to help their parents who lost upwards of 50 percent of their retirement in the crash of '08.

Outliving your retirement also puts your other assets at risk because say you had to move into assisted living or a nursing home? I have already noted how expensive long-term care really is. What if you don't have enough monthly income to handle the expense, but you own enough assets that you don't qualify for Medicaid? The government will take your income and your assets in something called a "spend down." You are not allowed to retain more than $1,500 a month in income and you cannot hold more than $2,000 in liquid assets. Your spouse can keep your home, but the government will also put a lien on it and take the funds from the home when it is sold to pay back the Medicaid account.[25] Is there any way to protect yourself from this threat?

Risk # 7 Premature death risk. At some point, we must all "shuffle off this mortal coil" as Hamlet so eloquently if sadly reminds us, but what happens if we die when we are too young? What happens to your family if you're the primary bread winner and you pass away? It's the first concern I have when I meet with families for the first time. If your affairs are in order, it makes the financial burden easier to bear on the family. Burial costs are very expensive, averaging around $8,500, but many spend more to comply with their loved one's wishes. I know one woman who spent $18,000 for her husband's funeral. The family wanted the casket to be wooden and nicely carved, and the wake afterwards was attended by close to three hundred people. It was the remainder of the account he had from a $50,000 inheritance he had put in mutual funds that had lost over half its value in '08.

However, what if the husband dies and leaves the wife with nothing but Social Security? When the bread-winner dies, his or her pension either is gone or reduced. The surviving spouse gets a cut in Social Security; they lose the smaller of the two checks.

If the deceased person was the stay-at-home mom, how much are they worth? Recently a video went viral about a husband who calculated how much it would cost him to replace his wife. Between child care, chauffeuring duties, being the maid and the chef, and often being the home's finance manager, he figured it up to be $72,000.

Death is inevitable. Premature death is one of the sharper arrows that can be flung at your loved ones.

Risk #8: Inflation

There is one more category of risk that is a class all by itself and affects every other risk mentioned. It is perhaps the most threatening of all to your retirement savings: inflation. It is the process of continuously rising prices in the wake of the continuously falling value of money. It means that your dollars don't stretch as far as they used to and that's why it's also called purchasing power risk in some circles. While the other life risks hit unexpectedly, this is the risk that is ever present and ever growing in everyone's life.

The government has changed the way it calculates inflation more than twenty times in thirty years. This is important for you to know because they usually make it look a lot better than it actually is.[26] The government does that so it doesn't have to spend as much on "cost of living adjustments," which means that even though common sense will tell you that the price you pay for eggs this year is less than the price you will pay for eggs next year, the government doesn't officially recognize that. This means your Social Security, for example, is based on a lower cost of living than what is actually true.

Inflation affects all of us and in a myriad of ways. The experts are pretty clear that even "small changes in life expectancies"—meaning how long you live—can create solvency issues for your pension plans including 401(k)s and IRAs. Solvency issues mean how much money you have left to take out. We covered that in longevity risk. But the real problem is, how far is your planned income going to carry you through month to month? Is your monthly income going to be able to cover the cost of your heating bill, your health insurance, your house taxes, your phone, cable, internet—all the amenities that we have come to take for granted? If you no longer live in the house you paid for, you'll have rent and of course food. Your income may cover it all now, but what about in twenty years?

Inflation is perhaps the scariest of all risks—it's the one you absolutely cannot control. Financial planners try all sorts of ways to alleviate that risk. They may talk about TIPS (U.S. Treasury Inflation-Protected Security) and Stable Value funds—words and concepts that sound good, but do they adhere to the family financial principles? Robert C. Merton, in *The Harvard Business Review,* makes it pretty clear: our standard of living in retirement should be measured first by how much income we need, then by how much money we have socked away, for the two, he says, are not always related.[27]

Life is full of risks. Catastrophic illness or accidents will happen—even when you're healthy. You will either lose your job or change careers at least once in your life. We can run away from risks or pretend they don't exist, but that doesn't solve anything. Risk can be mitigated, and sometimes even eliminated, but only when you face up to the realities that are present. Only then can you take an objective look at what can truly protect you from them.

To find a local Family Financial Miracle Representative, please visit www.FFMRegistry.com.

—PART TWO—
My Family Financial Miracle

I always love watching how my wife handles our daughter. She is now a teenager—smart, savvy, and as all teenagers are, impressionable. One day I overheard Monica helping our daughter and her friend handle some situation about peer pressure. She told the girls what every mother should tell her child: people want you to do things their way because either that's what they're comfortable with or it benefits them in some way. Then she said something that I thought was pretty profound: to overcome peer pressure, you have to play out the consequences of your decisions in your mind and base your decision on the outcome you're most comfortable with.

Over the years, I have asked a lot of people what they think would make up the perfect financial product to handle their money. They inevitably give me this list:

- I want it to earn a good rate of return
- I want it not to be taxed
- I want to have access to my money any time I want it
- I want it safe—I do not want to risk losing my money
- I don't want the government controlling my money (meaning limiting when I can have access to my money or when I have to distribute my money).

People also want to be able to

- Contribute as much money into their savings vehicles as they want when they want
- Have life risks handled like long-term care or protection from job loss.

Finally, they want their contributions deductible from taxes—401(k)s and IRAs taught them that.

These benefits really are the holy grail of benefits for a financial product. Think about it—pretty much everything you do or buy has a holy grail. Whether it is a car or a house, you have an ideal of what you want in your mind, and you're not happy until you find it. You might have a really good sales person convince you that their product has everything you really want, but when it doesn't—when the promise doesn't play out in real terms—you probably get more than a little grumpy.

Money management and financial savings vehicles are no different in this way. The ideal does exist. The product I'm about to show you delivers on every one of the benefits I listed above except one, but to really understand how it works, you'll need to look past what you think you know, and what others—like TV personalities and your next-door neighbor—think.

In other words, you're going to have to "just say no" to the pressure your peers and many others will throw at you. Realize that the naysayers have an agenda: they tell you what they want you to do because, most likely, it benefits them in some way. I have an agenda too. I want your money to be as protected as mine has been over the years. So as I tell you what my family financial miracle is, play out the consequences of how this miracle may be able to help you ideally manage *your* money.

My money miracle is yours. It's up to you to decide if you're ready to accept the truth about what I discovered and enjoy knowing your money is preotected.

5 The Magic of True Compounding

When people first learn about the family financial miracle, they are either skeptical or dismissive. They can't believe that there is a wealth management vehicle that will give them all the benefits they want, but it can.

I remind them of the eight major financial risks: losing your money in the stock market or unexpectedly high taxation; the life risks that can suck your savings accounts dry including catastrophic illness, long term care needs, job loss, legal action, outliving your retirement, or premature death. When I mention inflation, pretty much everyone groans because they think of how much more money they're spending at the grocery store, and they feel like they really can't do anything about it.

I tell them my family financial miracle handles the risks *and* is the only product that handles all but one of the Holy Grail benefits of financial products.

Then I ask them what they think of life insurance. After they roll their eyes, they say: It's expensive. Its money I'm spending for my heirs that I don't get to use. This then prompts them to ask, "Isn't life insurance really death insurance?"

I pause. After a moment, I say, "My family financial miracle is life insurance."

They have the same reaction I'm sure you're having about now. You're thinking life insurance is so far away from the perfect financial product, you can't help but blurt out: "I've come all this way for *life insurance*?!"

Yes you have. And I suspect that when you find out that it really does make good on its promises, you're going to be very happy you stuck it through.

The first time I was presented with the idea of life insurance as a way to grow and protect my money, I was skeptical as well. I remember the day I walked into an insurance agent's office. He was selling whole life. He'd been referred to me by a friend who is in the insurance business who told me that a life insurance policy is *the* place to put my money. I didn't believe him. I basically had the same reaction you just did.

I also knew that I could walk out of that agent's office just as easily as I had the stock broker's. I decided to stay for two reasons: I already knew that insurance companies fared far better in economic downturns than other financial institutions like banks. That and since my experience with stock brokers had helped me forge my family financial principles, I knew I had a basis from which to test any financial vehicle, investment or otherwise.

I quickly discovered that the life insurance he was talking about isn't the kind that your grandfather had, the kind that made sure your grandmother had money once he was gone, but Granddad did not have access to any cash while he was alive. This type of life insurance still exists. We know it as "term" life insurance.

This kind of insurance is a commodity purchase. You're buying a death benefit for a set amount of money. You spend the least amount of money for the greatest amount of death benefit you can get. The policy expires after a certain amount of time, and there is no cash buildup that you can either extract out of the policy or borrow against. If you die within the time period specified by the policy (the term) then your beneficiary will receive the death benefit—the payout of the policy. It isn't worth anything other than that payout, and the payout only comes if the policy is in force when you pass away.

While term life insurance appears to be less expensive relative to permanent life insurance products, you *are* spending money for the sole benefit of your heirs. This is why many financial planners advise their clients to buy a term life insurance policy and invest the difference a permanent policy charges into a separate investment account.

The specific type of life insurance I found, the life insurance that is my family financial miracle, is different. It is a permanent life insurance contract called Index Universal Life, or IUL policy for short. It's "permanent" meaning it combines a death benefit with a savings account, which is called the "cash value" of the contract.

An Index Universal Life insurance policy is *not* classified as an investment, like a mutual fund—remember only licensed brokers are allowed to sell those and other stock and bond investments. According to the IRS codes, permanent cash value life insurance is there first to provide a financial resource to replace a financial loss of an individual or a couple in the case of premature death to a surviving heir. That's what makes it life insurance. The cash value component of the contract was designed to be a secondary benefit.

I knew about the death benefit of life insurance, and I understood the purpose. I had heard stories of widows who were so grateful when their insurance agent gave them a substantial check, what's called the death claim, after their husbands had died. They were also very appreciative of the fact that this money wasn't taxed. I also know people whose wives spent the remaining portion of their husband's retirement account on his funeral. Of course I wanted my family to be protected financially if I died unexpectedly. But I thought pretty much like everyone else did—life insurance was there for the death benefit, so the best way to buy it was to pay the least amount for the most amount of death benefit. We have been taught by the financial institutions that insurance is a needs-based product; I believe that it is a "want-product." It is the only product that can guarantee what I want to happen will happen.

It was the savings portion, the cash value, however, of the Index Universal Life that eluded me. It didn't take me long to realize that these IUL products were actually designed from the chassis up to be very efficient for optimizing growth of the cash inside the contract.

I knew enough about life insurance to say at that point, if I could grow my money safely and have all the other great benefits life insurance provides, the IUL might just be the kind of financial planning product I needed.

How Can Money Grow?

Index Universal Life contracts are not the easiest thing to understand. They have a lot of moving parts, and because they are potentially so powerful, they are also regulated by their own IRS rules. For example, in an IUL policy, you don't make annual deposits into the policy, you pay annual premiums. There are rules that must be followed that dictate when the money can go into the policy and how much at any given time. That's what IRS code 7702 governs. I'll get to all that in the next chapter.

The first and most important thing to know about an IUL contract is how your money grows. My biggest gripe with all the traditional financial vehicles is that even though your money may grow well sometimes, it is also exposed to the market losses that inevitably happen. In other words, it's not protected. The IUL, on the other hand, allows your money to grow while keeping it safe. This is always good, so I went about finding out how that all works.

The Value of True Compounding

Step one to growing your money is understanding that with the IUL you get something called "true compounding." Compounding is a process whereby the value of an account is always increasing over time because the interest is calculated on the initial principal and also on the accumulated interest. It's interest on interest, and it will make a deposit grow faster because you're making money on your principal *and* interest every year. Here's an easy chart to see how compounding works based on an initial deposit of $100 with a static or fixed interest rate of 10 percent that compounds yearly:

Initial deposit:	$100
Year one interest earned:	$10
New principal:	$110 (principal plus interest)
Year two interest earned	$11
New principal:	$121 (principal plus interest)
Year three interest earned:	$12.10
New principal:	$133.10 (principal plus interest)

In a "true" compounding environment, you never lose any value. The principal on which interest is calculated for the current compounding period is the sum of the principal and interest from the previous period. That's great, but the important thing is, it's true compounding because you never sustain a loss.

Compounding, in its purest form, means you're earning interest every year, no matter what. There are financial products, like CD's, that do exactly that. They have a fixed or static rate of return. You're making a certain percentage every year on your money, and you never, ever lose the balance in your account. But you can also have a true compounding environment when you have the upside potential of the stock market with a mechanism in place that guarantees no losses when the stock market has one of its inevitable corrections.

If the possibility to lose money in the market exists, you are in a variable or speculative environment with usually no safety net. This is not a true compounding environment. Compounding interest is your friend; it never allows an account to go backwards. This is why the old adage: "he who understands it earns it; he who doesn't pays it," is true. Compounding interest is a factor used in growing money as well as borrowing money and banks use compounding interest on loans and credit cards. You earn more efficiently when you have your money in a compounding environment, but you pay more for a loan that is in a compounding environment as well.

I remember reading about true compounding in *Money* magazine when I was in my early thirties. That is where I first learned that Albert Einstein supposedly said it is the eighth wonder of the world. It's almost a cliché to say, but it is a strong comment. To me, it is the *only* way you can truly grow your money. The article showed a comparison of an initial deposit that was subject to variable rates of return from the stock market versus a static or fixed rate of return. It was clear to see that losing money, like in a market downturn, was detrimental to the compounding-interest curve.

Let me show you what this looks like using a $100,000 initial deposit. The first chart is the same one I used in chapter 2. It shows the variable rates of return based on the price of the S&P 500 from 2000 to 2014:

Variable Rates of Return

Year	S&P Return %	Account Value
2000	-10.14	$89,860
2001	-13.04	$78,142
2002	-23.37	$59,880
2003	26.38	$75,676
2004	8.99	$82,479
2005	3.00	$84,953
2006	13.62	$96,524
2007	3.53	$99,931
2008	-38.49	$61,468
2009	23.45	$75,882
2010	12.78	$85,580
2011	1.00	$86,436
2012	13.41	$98,027
2013	29.60	$127,043
2014	11.39	$141,513
15 Yr Tot	**2.34%**	**$141,513**

When an account goes into the negative like this one, you know you are not in a true compounding environment. Rather, you're working with accrued interest in a speculative environment with variable returns. It's the roller coaster of speculation in chapter 2: when you have a negative balance in any year, it takes a while, too long if you ask me, to regain your losses.

Now, let's take a look at what happens when you have a fixed or static rate of return that compounds yearly based on the average rate of return that you got in the market from 2000 to 2014: 2.34 percent.

Fixed Rate of Return

Yr	BOY Balance	Fix ROR	Index Yr	Ann Gain/Loss	EOY Balance
1	$100,000	2.34%	2000	$2,340	$102,340
2	$102,340	2.34%	2001	$2,395	$104,735
3	$104,735	2.34%	2002	$2,451	$107,186
4	$107,186	2.34%	2003	$2,508	$109,694
5	$109,694	2.34%	2004	$2,567	$112,261
6	$112,261	2.34%	2005	$2,627	$114,887
7	$114,887	2.34%	2006	$2,688	$117,576
8	$117,576	2.34%	2007	$2,751	$120,327
9	$120,327	2.34%	2008	$2,816	$123,143
10	$123,143	2.34%	2009	$2,882	$126,024
11	$126,024	2.34%	2010	$2,949	$128,973
12	$128,973	2.34%	2011	$3,018	$131,991
13	$131,991	2.34%	2012	$3,089	$135,080
14	$135,080	2.34%	2013	$3,161	$138,241
15	$138,241	2.34%	2014	$3,235	$141,475

Your ending account balance in the compounding environment versus the speculative environment is roughly the same, but your money is growing at a consistent, steady, compounding rate.

True compounding is much less stressful. If all else is equal, meaning you're not taxed, you don't have any fees or costs for anything, you make the same amount either way.

To look at it a bit differently, this chart shows you a line graph of the same thing. It shows the average rate of return in the S&P 500 from 2005 to 2014 (the last ten years not the last fifteen):

Compounding and Consistency are the Keys to Growth

Yr	Compounding ROR	Compounding EOY Balance	Market Returns ROR	Market Returns EOY Balance	Difference
1	5.45%	$105,450	3.00%	$103,000	$2,450
2	5.45%	$111,197	13.62%	$117,029	-$5,832
3	5.45%	$117,257	3.53%	$121,160	-$3,903
4	5.45%	$123,648	-38.49%	$74,525	$49,123
5	5.45%	$130,387	23.45%	$92,002	$38,385
6	5.45%	$137,493	12.78%	$103,759	$33,734
7	5.45%	$144,986	0.00%	$103,759	$41,227
8	5.45%	$152,888	13.41%	$117,673	$35,215
9	5.45%	$161,220	29.60%	$152,505	$8,715
10	5.45%	$170,007	11.39%	$169,875	$132

Compounding and Consistency Bring Peace of Mind

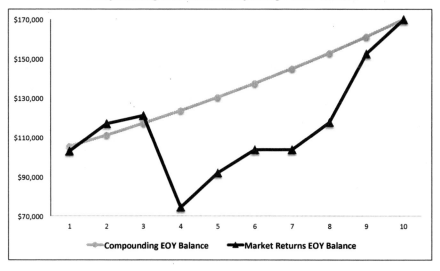

Let me ask you. If you knew you were going to end up in the same place, what would you rather live through: the ups and down of speculation with your money or the nice smooth road of true compounding? I suspect you'd take the smooth ride every time because it's far less nerve-racking. I know my wife likes it when I'm less stressed. I sleep better, and that keeps the doctor away. This is why I think true compounding is one of the greatest inventions in history.

How Do You Want Your Money to Grow?

Step two of the growing-your-money process has to do with why the word "index" is in Index Universal Life.

As the IUL contract is being funded, and as it continues through its entire life cycle, it has two crediting methods for cash accumulation:

- a fixed account that credits a static crediting rate that is determined at the annual anniversary of the contract, or
- The Index crediting options that allows an allocation of all or a portion of the cash inside the policy to mirror an equity index.

Fixed

We have covered the idea of a fixed crediting method above with the true compounding. You have the option in an IUL to put your money in an environment that is fixed. It's usually around 4 to 5 percent. It is very conservative but very safe, and this is what it looks like with an initial deposit of $100,000.

Fixed Rate of Return

Year	Return %	Account Value
2000	4.00%	$104,000
2001	4.00%	$108,160
2002	4.00%	$112,486
2003	4.00%	$116,985
2004	4.00%	$121,664
2005	4.00%	$126,531
2006	4.00%	$131,592
2007	4.00%	$136,856
2008	4.00%	$142,330
2009	4.00%	$148,023
2010	4.00%	$153,944
2011	4.00%	$160,102
2012	4.00%	$166,506
2013	4.00%	$173,166
2014	4.00%	$180,093
15 Yr Tot	4.00%	$180,093

You're only making 4 percent, but because you're not going backwards, you come out of the fifteen years making $80,093 on your initial deposit. That isn't a bad deal. Furthermore, there is no risk. You know what the value of your money is going to be in ten, twenty, even forty years if you leave it in for that long. In a variable or speculative environment, you don't know what your future account value will be, and this creates uncertainty for planning for the future. You could make 2.34 percent or 23.4 percent.

You have already seen what happens to your money when it's in the stock market. Here's the chart again from the S&P 500 for the past fifteen years:

Variable Rates of Return

Year	Return %*	Account Value
2000	-10.14	$89,860
2001	-13.04	$78,142
2002	-23.37	$59,880
2003	26.38	$75,676
2004	8.99	$82,479
2005	3.00	$84,953
2006	13.62	$96,524
2007	3.53	$99,931
2008	-38.49	$61,468
2009	23.45	$75,882
2010	12.78	$85,580
2011	1.00	$86,436
2012	13.41	$98,027
2013	29.60	$127,043
2014	11.39	$141,513
15 Yr Tot	**2.34%**	**$141,513**

*These returns represent the S&P 500 price and do not include dividends.

Notice that the 4 percent fixed account made about $40,000 more in fifteen years than it would have made in the market for the same period of time. Granted, the past fifteen years are historically some of the worst years in the market, but if you watched your account balances rise and fall during these years, you can start to appreciate the beauty in this.

Indexing

The way to get the predictability and protection from loss while still enjoying the upside potential of the speculative market happens when you choose the index allocation for all or part of your cash value.

I have already talked about stock indices in part one in terms of one of the most well-known, the S&P 500. S&P stands for Standard and Poor's. The Dow Jones Industrial is another very familiar index; it is actually the oldest stock index and was created by Charles Dow, also the founder of *The Wall Street Journal.* These indices measure the average performance of a number of designated stocks at any given time on any given day the stock market is open. The S&P 500 measures five hundred of America's largest corporations based on profit. The Dow measures a set of thirty public companies in the U.S., all of them "blue chip"—financially fit companies with dependable performance like General Electric and Walt Disney.

A stock market index measures the price changes of the specified group of stocks. When you hear "the S&P jumped ten points today," that means the value of the stocks in that index went up that day by a certain percentage amount; however, the current level of the index has no dollar value correlation. How those points are figured is complicated and is based on the value of the stocks and the percentage of increase or decrease. What's important is insurance companies use the value of the index to calculate the amount they are going to credit your account for that year. In 2014, the S&P's average performance was 11.39. That is the percentage an indexed contract could credit, and thus the cash value of your policy increased by that percentage for that year.

However, it is important to note that the cash value of your policy is not actually participating in the market. The insurance company does not invest your money in any stock or bond. Again, the stock market indices are used by life insurance companies as the measure of how much to credit your account for that year.

Now, if you're asking yourself, even if your money isn't in the market, how can you eliminate the risk if the percentage of interest you're making is tied to stock market index returns? It has to do with two governing components in the indexing portion of an IUL policy called the cap and floor. The cap allows you the participation in market-like returns. The floor is the mechanism in place that guarantees no losses, thus keeping you in the true compounding environment.

The Safety Net

The "floor" is the safety net built into the indexing portion of an IUL. It is set, by contract, usually at 0 percent. This means that your money will be protected; it will never suffer a negative rate of return. If the stock market dips or tanks, your money isn't going to go along with it.

Let's say the index you choose to track your cash against each year is the S&P index. It dips a negative 13.04 percent like it did in 2001. Do you lose your money? No. Your cash value doesn't participate in the market loss. It doesn't earn any interest that year, but hey, if you had the choice of making zero earnings on your money or losing roughly $10,000 of your $100,000 in 2001, which would you choose? Pretty much everyone I talk to chooses zero earnings every time.

The floor that's set in an IUL is a nice and conservative feature. When you compare market performance against an IUL with a floor of zero for our benchmark 2000 to 2014, this is what you get:

Comparison Between S&P Price and IUL with a Floor (0) and Cap (12)

Yr	S&P Ret %	Acct Value	Cap & Floor	IUL Acct Value
2000	-10.14%	$89,860	0.00%	$100,000
2001	-13.04%	$78,142	0.00%	$100,000
2002	-23.37%	$59,880	0.00%	$100,000
2003	26.38%	$75,676	12.00%	$112,000
2004	8.99%	$82,479	8.99%	$122,069
2005	3.00%	$84,953	3.00%	$125,731
2006	13.62%	$96,524	12.00%	$140,819
2007	3.53%	$99,931	3.53%	$145,790
2008	-38.49%	$61,468	0.00%	$145,790
2009	23.45%	$75,882	12.00%	$163,285
2010	12.78%	$85,580	12.00%	$182,879
2011	1.00%	$86,436	1.00%	$184,708
2012	13.41%	$98,027	12.00%	$206,873
2013	29.60%	$127,043	12.00%	$231,698
2014	11.39%	$141,513	11.39%	$258,088
15 Yr Tot	2.34%	$141,513	6.52%	$258,088

Starting in 2000, the stock market tanked for the first three years. If you made an initial $100,000 investment in the market that year, you suffered losses each year in the stock market—a little over $40,000 when it was all said and done. The next five years, the market shows positive gains but because you lost so much, you still haven't recovered. When the disaster happened in 2008, you lost even more. But if you look at the IUL side, you don't lose a dime for the first three years. You haven't made any, but you haven't lost any. That's the safety net.

The Cap

Now here's where it gets fun. Look at year four. On the stock market side, you've made back $25,000 of the $40,000 loss. On the IUL side, you've made 12 percent. In fact, over the course of fifteen years, you made 12 percent six times. That is the cap, the provision in the IUL contract that regulates the maximum gains you can earn in any given year. It is based on a market index. So in the example above, when the market rebounds 26.38 percent, you earn 12 percent. Your $100,000, of which you never lost any in the market corrections, is now worth $112,000, and since this is a true compounding environment, the interest you earn the next year is calculated on the sum of the base principal and the interest earned. This total amount is now classified as your new principal, guaranteed never to be subject to market loss. So in year five, you make 8.99 percent on the $112,000.

The cap is determined on an annual basis and is predicated on how well the economy is doing and how well the insurance carrier's general account is performing. I will explain this general account later in the book because it has everything to do with how the insurance company can guarantee rates of return, and why I said in the introduction that the miracle I found is backed by one of the most powerful and reliable institutions on earth. Over the past fifteen years, the IUL caps have been as high as 17 percent and as low as 8 percent.

In the above example, the cap is set at twelve (a realistic cap based on current capped percentages). It is hypothetical because the caps can move from year to year and are different in various contracts, but this shows you what is possible with a 12 percent cap. If the market index increases eight percent for the year, you get credited 8 percent. If the cap is twelve and the market credits 1 percent, then you make 1 percent that year. But if the cap is 12 percent and the index credits 14 percent, or even 12.78 percent as it did in 2001, your account is credited 12 percent. If the market does exceptionally well, as it did in 2013 with a 29.60 gain, and your cap is twelve, you earn 12 percent interest.

Some people will ask, "But why would I want to earn only 12 percent when I could earn 28 or more if the market is good?" Because they are forgetting the all-important floor.

Look at 2008. The market crashes a negative 38.49 percent, but your money in an IUL loses nothing because you have a guaranteed zero percent floor. If your $100,000 was in the market from 2000 onwards, it was just about back to the original deposit when the crash of '08 sent it spiraling back almost $30,000.

The IUL policy is designed to protect you from market losses while giving you a competitive rate of return. The price you pay for this protection is you will not participate in 100 percent of the unusual market gains above the cap. In this particular fifteen year period, the market goes above the cap six times and below zero four times. Remember that when you lose, it takes longer to recover. If you have a zero floor, you don't have to work to regain your money. It's a trade-off that most people are willing to make.

The cap and floor in an IUL creates more predictability, more stability, and less stress. It's a safe, conservative environment. You get to enjoy the upside potential of the market, but you're not going to participate in the uncertainty of the losses. No one can predict what the market is going to do. When I am working between a floor and a cap, I know I have a security blanket. It's my peace of mind. Why? The numbers work: without taking into consideration any cost on either side of this comparison, no loads, management fees, taxation, or mortality cost between 2000 and 2014, if I put $100,000 in the speculative market, I would have a balance of $141, 513. If I had my money in an IUL, I would have over one hundred thousand dollars more with a total balance of $258,088.

Lock and Reset

The cap and floor is your first line of protection against market loss. But insurance companies, being the conservative institutions that they are, have put in place another layer of protection for your money in an IUL contract: the lock-in of annual gains and reset of the annual index value.

For example let's say you have a zero floor and a cap of twelve.

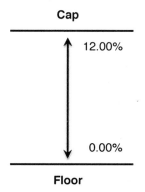

Cap

12.00%

0.00%

Floor

If the start date of my IUL contract is today, and the S&P 500 index is currently valued at 2,100 (that's what the S&P is trading at) my start value would be 2100 for the year. This time next year the insurance company would compare this year's current value of the S&P index to next year's S&P value. If the index goes up 10 percent to 2310, the policy would credit the increase in the value up to the policy cap. In the chart below, you can see $100,000 going up 10 percent or $10,000. Once the policy is credited, your gains are locked in. Your accumulated cash is protected and becomes the principal for the next year's crediting cycle.

If at the end of the next year, the S&P index value dropped 10 percent to 2079, the IUL policy would credit zero percent because the S&P index dropped below what you started at. However, you have not lost any of your money. Your principal remains the same as the previous year.

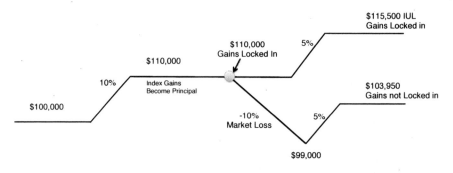

How Reset Works

Now here's how the reset comes into play. Continuing the example above: the S&P index value is at 2079. That is my policy's new starting value for the next year, and this new value is the point from where my gains are calculated for the next twelve months. I'm not starting at 2100, the value from my first year. Rather, I get to start where the market left off on my policy's anniversary date.

If the S&P index value drops 30 percent to 1455, my account balance remains at $110,000. If the S&P index value shoots up 20 percent the next year to 1746, my policy will be credited the 12 percent cap. Now here is what's so powerful about the reset feature in an IUL policy: my policy balance, which didn't lose anything when the market crashed 30 percent, gets the benefit of the big market jump because the starting value for the year is 1455. Here's what that looks like:

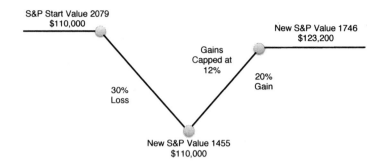

Because the insurance company resets the index value every year, you have the opportunity to always participate in the upside movement of the market. Without it, you are at the mercy of the market roller coaster. With it, you don't participate in any of the market downturns, and because the index value is resetting every year, when the market rebounds (and it usually does when there is a major market correction), you get to enjoy earning interest up to the entire policy index cap.

The index value resets every year in the policy, and it is why your money grows uninterrupted in a true compounding environment.

To view a live demonstration of caps and floors/lock-in and reset, please visit www.myfamilyfinancialmiracle.com/video.

Mix and Match

There is one more aspect to how you can manage your money inside of an IUL. In most IUL contracts, you can mix and match how much money you want to put in a fixed rate of return allocation, and how much you want to put in an equity index allocation. If you think the market is not going to do well in any given year, you can have all your money earning a fixed rate of return. You can put it all back in the indexed allocation the next year when the market rebounds. Or you can do a percentage of each: 25 percent in the fixed and 75 percent in the indexed or a 30 percent/70 percent split. You get to choose. This allows you to be in the driver's seat with your money—and control is just as important as safety in my mind.

The floor and cap provisions, along with the annual lock-in and reset feature in an IUL contract keeps the cash value of these contracts either making money or protecting the principal. Once the annual interest is credited to the principal, the balance becomes the new principal, never to be subject to loss. That's what the insurance agent I met told me, and it played out when I ran the numbers.

I also quickly learned as I studied various IUL contracts that not all contracts are created equal. For example, the cap is different for different companies and different products. Depending on the insurance company, you could have a set cap or no cap at all. I've seen caps set as low as 8 percent, which means that no matter what the market does from year to year, your cap is only 8 percent. I also know companies that don't set a limit on the cap, meaning the cap is determined by the yearly performance of the stock market. So it follows that the higher the cap, the higher the average your compounding interest will be. Just like there are poorly made cars, middle of the road type vehicles, and high performance machines, IULs can be poorly designed, decent, or high performance.

———◆———

I studied the products. I've had other clients study the IUL contracts. We all came to the same conclusion. Once we see how safe our money can be and how the cash value of the policy can grow at a very competitive rate because it is tied to the market gains without participating directly in market volatility, we are all very happy.

I remember thinking when I understood that portion of the IUL, so far, so good: two of the three family financial principle rings connect up in the IUL.

I was pretty happy about that, but what about the other benefit—namely income with liquidity, use, and control—that I not only wanted but found necessary for success?

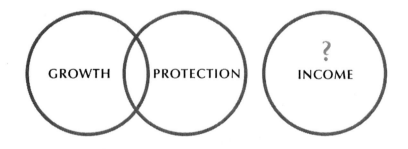

To find a local Family Financial Miracle Representative, please visit www.FFMREgistry.com.

6 Making the IRS Work for You

When I visited the life insurance agent who introduced me to a Universal Index Life contract, he explained to me that there are IRS codes that direct how IUL contracts work, and these codes or rules are very similar to the codes that manage IRAs. They regulate how much money can go in at any given time and how you can distribute the cash build-up inside the policy tax-free.

I thanked him and walked out, scratching my head. What financial savings instrument allowed you to take *out* money in a tax favored way? I knew from my experience with qualified plans, you could put money in tax-deferred and even grow it that way, but take it out with little or no tax consequences? I needed more information, but now I had something useful to work with. If the IRS had made a tax code for it, it must be really important.

When I want to know about anything, I turn into a Bloodhound, sniffing out every last piece of data I can find. The first thing I did was search on Amazon for "7702." I didn't find that much except a big blue book that cost $160. I thought, are you kidding me? But I bought it because if I was going to put in hundreds of thousands of dollars into a life insurance policy, I better really figure out how it all worked.

The further into the book I read, the more I realized I was reading the instruction manual on how product developers in insurance companies build IUL contracts. It was full of actuarial tables—the tables that list out the probability of someone dying by their next birthday—as well as a lot of common sense. I kept thinking, if the IRS has a manual this comprehensive on how to construct life insurance policies, there must be a whole lot more to it than what we see on the surface.

To make sure I knew what I was looking at on paper, I got a hold of as many IUL contracts from different insurance companies as I could. There were three basic types, and they all started sounding like the information from the book I bought. Some of the contracts had good provisions, some didn't. I talked to life insurance carriers and then to agents who sold IULs. I wanted to know how well the IUL had performed for their clients. I learned that very few agents were selling the IUL because they were a great way to grow wealth. They were selling them as typical life insurance—for the death benefit.

I came to the conclusion after all my research that the Index Universal Life policy is a fantastic savings vehicle. It really did all the things it promised; the problem was some of the agents selling them didn't fully understand how they worked. The trick I found lay in how you actually build the policy. You could either build it to benefit your heirs or you could build it to grow your money, and to know the difference is to know the basics of two IRS codes: 7702, which tells you how much money you can put in and how often and 72(e) which dictates how the money can be taken out.

The Secret to 7702

The Internal Revenue Code Section 7702 provides the rules that dictate and regulate the insurance industry's product development teams. These rules were written to restrict as much as possible how the policy is funded, including how quickly money can be put into a permanent life insurance contract as well as the buildup of cash inside of it.

IRS code 7702 is extensive, and most will wonder why the IRS would go to so much trouble to create such an in-depth code to manage a life insurance contract. The simple answer is that cash accumulated inside a permanent life insurance contract grows tax deferred, you can distribute it at your discretion tax-free, and the death benefit will go to an heir completely income-tax free. These features are a big concern of the IRS for abuse. When they are concerned, they regulate. It seems when our government gets involved in managing anything, they tend to make something simple as complicated as possible.

One of the most misunderstood aspects of IRS code 7702 hovers around how much and how quickly you can put funds into an IUL contract. I am going to walk you through the process because it is actually a quick lesson on life insurance.

As I have noted, most people approach the purchase of life insurance already knowing how much death benefit they want to buy. So they shop around to find the least amount they have to spend to pay for the amount of insurance they want. If you're buying life insurance this way, your primary concern is to provide a financial benefit to your heirs if premature death occurs. However, to use an IUL policy to grow your cash, you have to think backwards, reverse engineer the policy structure. Instead of determining how much life insurance you want to purchase and having the insurance company then figure out the amount of the annual premium, you start with the amount of premium, *total*, you want to put into the policy and figure out the death benefit based on that amount.

Here's how I explained it to my builder who built my home in Virginia Beach. It's a good-sized house. It cost a lot, so this builder is making a decent living.

I love my builder, but he's scattered. He can't stay focused very long before he's off on another subject. He lived through the 2008 crash, but he was scathed. I asked him where he was putting his money. He said the typical: IRA.

He knew what I did for a living. We had talked about life insurance before. I said, "You should put your savings in an IUL policy."

Because he can't sit still for more than thirty minutes, he said, "Just set it up."

I asked him how much he was willing to put away for retirement per year. He said, "I usually save $20,000." He was fifty-five at the time and wanted to retire at sixty-five.

Easy stuff. His total amount of premium would be $200,000: $20,000 each year for ten years. He was fine with that, but he did ask, "I know I can do $20,000 this year, but I don't know if I can do that next year or the next."

I told him it was up to him how much premium he wanted to put into the policy. The insurance company would tell me how much death benefit would match the premium.

He said, "Fine. Build it for $200,000. I'll figure out how to get the money." He was ready to move on to his next project.

All life insurance companies have a computer program that tells an agent the amount of death benefit based on the amount of premium paid or vice versa. When I entered in the builder's $200,000, the software program came back with a minimum death benefit of $910,000.

That's when I got his attention. He said, "Wait. Why am I paying for a million dollars' worth of life insurance to put away this $200,000? Why aren't we using something that doesn't have the cost of insurance involved in it? I don't need that much life insurance now, and I really don't need it when I retire."

I told him, "I don't know of any financial vehicle where you can put $200,000 away that gets you the ability to earn the upside potential of the market without participating in the losses and that allows you to grow the money tax deferred and take it out tax-free without the $910,000 death benefit. Why would you question the death benefit, which is going to someone you care about if you die prematurely, if it was just coming along for the ride anyway? The death benefit is what classifies this as a life insurance policy. If it wasn't there, this would be an investment, not life insurance, and then we wouldn't even be talking because I'm not an investment broker."

That made sense to him, so I continued.

"Okay listen. The amount of the death benefit is not me just pulling numbers out of the air. For this financial vehicle to be classified as life insurance, we *have* to comply with the IRS codes and federal law that dictates not only the amount of the death benefit based on the total amount of premium you're putting in but how often and how much you can put in at one time."

He could understand that, but he still needed more. So I showed him the following:

"Let's say you need a $500,000 death benefit to make your life insurance policy work for you. The insurance company has a minimum and a maximum premium that can be placed in the policy every year to make it a life insurance policy for a $500,000 death benefit. The minimum amount is $1,000; the maximum is $10,000. Who in your mind dictates or sets the minimum premium?"

"The insurance company does," was his response.

"You're right," I continued. "The minimum premiums pay just for the death benefit. This is basically term insurance. Now, who determines or sets the maximum of $10,000?"

"I don't know," he says.

"The government," I answer. "Why? Because any time the government puts a restriction on funding a financial product, it usually means the product favors the consumer, not so much the government. Furthermore, because the cash value in a life insurance policy is tax favored, the government is only going to give you so much room to work with."

To view a quick lesson on life insurance,
please visit www.myfamilyfinancialmiracle.com/video

I explained why. In the late 1970s/early 1980s, the government figured out people were using their life insurance policies as tax shelters. What they were doing was totally legal at the time, but people were putting hundreds of thousands as well as millions into these permanent life insurance policies all at once. The government rewrote the tax codes—7702—so that you had to spread out the maximum amount of premium you wanted to place in the policy, known as the Guideline Single Premium (GSP), over a period of time. The quickest that you could fund a permanent life insurance policy and still comply with 7702 and have tax favorability, is seven years, and it's called the 7-pay test.

In general it means the Guideline Single Premium must be broken into seven equal payments over seven years. If the policy is "max funded" (meaning the total Guideline Single Premium is in the policy), then it complies with the 7-pay test, and you can grow your money tax favored and access it tax-free.

The Modified Endowment Contract

There are other important stipulations in the IRS code about when you put money into your account. Say you were given $250,000 in an inheritance. You want to put it all in a life-insurance policy at one time. You can do that, but because it violates the 7-pay test, the life insurance policy changes to a single premium life insurance contract, which is also called a modified endowment contract or MEC for short. A MEC, because it fails to meet the 7-pay test, means that the policy is separated into its pure insurance portion, which is the death benefit, and the savings portion, the cash value.

If you "MEC" an insurance policy, it means that you have put too much money in too quickly. All the gains in the policy will now grow tax deferred, but all your gains will be taxed on distribution. When you access your money, you have to take the interest you earned first, and this will be taxed at your ordinary income-tax bracket. Once all the interest has been paid out of the policy, then your distributions will be on the basis (all the money you paid into the policy), and that money has already been taxed. Also, once a policy becomes a MEC, it cannot revert back to the tax advantages of a life insurance contract. This is why you want to be very careful and not accidentally MEC your policy. A MEC also has the same age restrictions as other qualified accounts, including a penalty if you withdraw money before you turn 59 ½ (unless you become disabled, then you can take it with no penalty).

There are some instances when a MEC makes sense, like when someone wants market-like potential with no risks but is in a low tax bracket. If that person puts all their savings in at one time, he or she can take advantage of seven years of compounding and that could outweigh the tax advantages.

Premium Flexibility

Let's get back to my builder. I told him that between the insurance-company minimum and government-mandated maximum amount of premium in a permanent life insurance contract, you have a whole lot of flexibility. The closer you get to the maximum every year, the quicker your money is going to grow because of the magic of true compounding. You can even push right up against the maximum premium every year and be okay. As long as it's within what is deemed allowable by the 7702 rules, you're good. You enjoy the tax benefits.

I then told my builder that the IUL has two added premium benefits: the first is the 7-pay test can be shortened to five years. So instead of taking seven years to fund the policy, it can be done in five. According to IRS rules, my builder's policy with the $200,000 Guideline Single Premium and death benefit of $910,000, allows him to put up to $40,000 a year for five years. He only wanted to put in $20,000, but he *could* put the maximum a year and keep the policy's status as an IUL contract.

An Indexed Universal Life policy also allows the policyholder flexibility in the way he or she puts the money in. While the 7-pay test says seven payments over seven years, in an IUL contract, once you make your first premium payment, the policy works under a cumulative total. Say your IUL contract has a $50,000 "face" (that means you have a $50,000 death benefit), and the amount of total premium you need to max fund it is $5,000. You can put in $1,000 each year for five years. But you could also pay $1,000 of your premium a year for the first two years, but in the third and fourth year you don't pay anything. That's okay. You're only earning interest on the $2,000 you've put in, but your policy hasn't cancelled. You can put in $1,000 in years five, six, and seven. Your total premium paid is $5,000. Your contract is funded; you're fine.

However, what happens if you pay $1,000 a year for the first three years but then decide to pay an additional $3,000? You have exceeded the maximum allowable amount for the 7-limit pay test. Your policy reverts to a MEC, and you cannot change it back. That's the limitation. It's not a huge one, but because it is based on IRS code, it cannot be changed.

This feature in an IUL policy is called flexible premium, and that is why the contracts I've been talking about are called Flexible Premium Indexed Universal Life. More to the point, these flexible premiums give you more control over your money because you decide what goes in and when.

Let me show you what my builder did so you have an example in real time. He started the policy February of 2009 with $20,000. Over the next twelve months, he put in another $1,250 a month, or $15,000. So his first year's total is $35,000. But remember, he can put up to $40,000 a year and keep the IUL status. In year two he put in another $15,000. But in year three, he was able to pay $70,000. He could, because he didn't make the full payments the previous two years. He can continue to pay $20,000 until he has the contract's total premium fully paid.

While 7702 restricts the amount of funds and how quickly the funds can be placed in the IUL contract, the annual restriction is not limited to a specified amount like with the IRA, 401(k) or other plans. While the IRS does restrict the amount of funds that a person can put into an IUL at any one time, the amount is based on the death benefit, not what the IRS says. So for most people IUL restrictions are a non-issue, whereas they can be with an IRA, ROTH IRA, or other qualified plans.

It doesn't matter how much or how little you want to put into a policy. If you can do a $200-a-month premium, fine. You can purchase an IUL with the appropriate death benefit attached. A portion of your premium is paying for the cost of insurance (which I cover in chapter 8), and the remaining money is either in a fixed or an indexed allocation earning interest with the caps and floors in place and your gains locked in with the index or interest rate resetting every year.

Tax Advantaged Distribution

Okay, let's check the family financial principles test. As I was researching all the stuff about premiums, I knew I liked the amount of control it gave me over my money, but it still didn't give me the final, stabilizing ring of income through liquidity, use, and control. I still didn't have the full shield in place because I didn't know how easily accessible my money was. If something happened to my wife or daughter, could I get my money relatively easy?

The answer is yes, and not just easily, but I could access my money tax-free. This happens because of the other IRS code that regulates permanent life insurance: 72(e). It dictates the different ways on how your money can be accessed within the policy.

The Money Buckets

There are two basic ways that you can take distributions on your IUL policy. To understand them, first visualize the IUL policy as a bucket that can hold money. Your age, sex, health condition, and the size of the death benefit are all factors that determine the amount of money your bucket can hold. The IRS statute 7702 makes the rules we must follow to determine the size of a bucket and how quickly you can fill it. It's full when the predetermined amount is met. For example, if a predetermined amount is $5,000 per year for ten years, the bucket would be built to only hold a total of $50,000 and no more. Remember, you can fill the bucket faster according to the IRS 7-pay rule but no faster.

When you place money into your policy, you are filling up the bucket towards its maximum limit. Once the maximum limit is met, you cannot put any more money in the policy unless you increase the death benefit or have some other "material change." But to keep things easy, let's say you're not going to increase the death benefit. In this case, only the annual interest credited will be allowed to continue to fill up the bucket once all the money you can contribute is met. This is called a maximum funded policy or maximum efficient policy.

At some point in time, preferably when the bucket is at maximum efficiency, you want to take money out of it. Your two choices, per IRS Code 72(e), are policy loans and the withdrawal-to-basis option.

Policy Loans

Most people, especially those who want to keep their money safe, have an adverse reaction to the word "loan." To them it means "debt," and no one likes debt. It took a bit of study for me to figure out how these policy loans work and how to use them to my advantage, but once I did, I knew policy loans inside these contracts were the final, wonderful feature that I needed for my money.

The typical IUL contract has two loan provisions: one is called a fixed loan and the other is called a Participating or Index loan. I'll get to the particulars of those in a moment. What made me sit up and pay attention was how you can pay the loan back. Both types of IUL policy loans offer something called "unstructured loan payments."

If you went to a bank and took out a $5,000 loan, you would be told what your payments are and when you have to pay them. You don't have a choice. But, what if you could take out a loan and decide when, how, and even *if* you wanted to pay it back? That's unstructured loan payments, and that is what makes the IUL policy loans a pretty sweet option.

When you take a policy loan from your life contract, you have the option to pay back the loan, pay just the annual interest on the loan, or never pay it back. If you chose to never pay back the loan, the borrowed dollars and the accumulated interest on the loan is paid back to the insurance carrier from the death benefit when you pass away. Here's an example. You have been diligent with your premium payments. After fifteen years, let's say your IUL has a cash value of $100,000. You take out a policy loan of $50,000. You decide that it will put you in financial distress to pay it back, so you don't. When you pass away, the death benefit is *less* the amount of the loan plus the interest owed to the insurance company. So if the death benefit is $500,000, your heirs will receive $50,000 less plus whatever amount of interest has accrued. If the interest is $10,000, then your beneficiaries will receive a $440,000 tax free benefit.

Participating Index Loan

The cash build up inside an Index UL insurance contract is in a true compounding environment—we already covered that in the previous chapter, but here's a quick review: say you chose the indexed option for cash accumulation. You have a 0 percent floor and 12 percent cap. You know you're not going to lose any money in a market crash, and you're going to make up to 12 percent depending on how well the market performs.

What does the crediting method have to do with the distribution of the money through a participating index loan? Everything. When you distribute funds from an IUL using a participating loan, the rate the insurance company charges on the distribution should be a fixed contractual percentage rate; if it is not, then the distribution is not a preferred participating loan provision.

When a distribution is made from an IUL policy as a loan, the amount of the distribution will come from the insurance company's general operating account. This is important because the money is *not* coming from the IUL policy's cash value. You're taking a loan out against the money in your policy. In other words, you are collateralizing the cash in your bucket, but the money in your bucket stays put, which means it is earning interest based on the indexing rules.

> To learn more about policy loan collateralization,
> please visit www.myfamilyfinancialmiracle.com/video.

This is where things get interesting. The policy loan from the insurance company's general account will charge a contractual rate, usually around 5 percent. If you borrow $10,000 against the cash value of your bucket, the interest the insurance company charges is $500 per year. However, the premium in your IUL along with the interest earned is still in the bucket. All the cash in your IUL will continue to operate in the 0 percent floor and 12 percent cap indexed environment (if that's what the cap was for that year).

The insurance company is charging you 5 percent interest on your loan, but let's say the market index credited 7 percent for that year. Yes, you're paying 5 percent to the insurance company for the amount of money you borrowed, but you've just made 7 percent on *all* the money in your policy. The money you borrowed (say the $10,000), still earned a positive rate of return of 7 percent, or $700 dollars. It's called positive arbitrage, and to me it's one of the most powerful features of the Index UL contract.

Fixed Loan

The other loan option available for distributing funds from an IUL contract is the fixed loan provision. This contractual provision allows the owner of the policy to take out a loan against the cash value through a fixed policy or zero spread loan. It is called "zero spread" because the insurance carrier will charge the same rate on the borrowed funds as they credit to the portion of the policy's cash value that is borrowed.

A typical fixed loan rate on an Index UL contract is between 2 percent and 6 percent. This rate is part of the product design and is disclosed as part of the policy's contractual loan provisions. I will use a 4 percent fixed loan rate to explain how this type of loan works.

If I had $100,000 in my policy's cash value, and I wanted to borrow $10,000 against that cash value using the policy's fixed loan provision, the insurance company would send me $10,000. That money is still taken from the insurance company's general fund, not from the cash value of my policy, but there has to be a corresponding amount allocated from my bucket to a guaranteed fixed loan account.

So $10,000 of my $100,000 of cash value would be segregated from my bucket. It doesn't matter if I have the entire $100,000 in an S&P index allocation or if I have my cash allocated in the insurance company's fixed account, $10,000 of the cash would be moved to a guaranteed fixed loan account. This loan account credits the $10,000 borrowed funds with a 4 percent annual interest rate. At the same time, the insurance company is charging 4 percent interest on the borrowed funds—hence a zero spread.

The fixed loan option is the more conservative loan option of the two. If you understand the benefits of the lock-in and reset feature with a cap and floor, you choose the participating loan option. Say you're charged 5 percent interest, but if the market has a down year, the cash value borrowed could earn 0 percent interest. This leaves you with a negative "spread" or cost of 5 percent. However, just the opposite can happen. The loan charge is 5 percent, and the Index goes up and caps at 12 percent. This creates a 7 percent positive return on the borrowed funds (12 percent positive rate of return minus the 5 percent charge.)

What is nice about the Index Universal Life contract is you can pick and choose which one of these loan provisions you want to use annually. You can use a fixed loan provision for distribution one year and switch to the participating loan next year, or visa a versa. Again, this makes this financial product one of the most flexible accumulation products available on the market.

Withdrawal-to-Basis Option

Rule 72(e) also stipulates that you don't have to take a policy loan. You can take distributions directly from your bucket using something called the "withdrawal-to-basis" option. This option allows you to withdraw all your premiums paid into the policy first before you ever would use a loan provision to access your gains. It's called FIFO—"first in first out"—and it works this way: If you paid premiums of $10,000 per year for ten years to completely fund a policy, and a few years later your IUL cash value grew to $160,000, your basis in this policy is $100,000 and your gain is $60,000. You can then systematically distribute the $100,000 basis first, without taxation. This leaves the gains inside the contract to continue to grow as you withdraw the basis. Once the basis has been dissipated, you then can either use one of the loan provisions in the contract to continue to distribute funds from the IUL completely tax-free, or you can systematically withdraw the gains. If you choose the latter you will have to pay your current income tax rate on the annual withdrawals.

You don't get this advantage with a MEC, by the way. A Modified Endowment Contract follows the LIFO rule of distribution, meaning Last in First Out. As with qualified plans, you have to take the interest credited to the policy out first. It is the money that has gone into the contract last. As per tax rules on earned interest, you have to pay taxes on that money when you distribute it. Once all the interest is gone from a MEC contract, then the basis or the money you paid into the contract can be distributed without taxation (because it went into the policy already taxed). A MEC contract also has a policy loan provision, but you have to pay taxes on the loan.

This is why you want to follow the rules and keep your policy an Index Universal Life; it keeps you in tax-free distribution for as long as possible.

Options for Withdrawal

The question then becomes when and why would someone use the withdrawal-to-basis provision over the loan provision and vice-versa. Options are good. They're even better if you understand the advantages your choices provide. You need to determine the purpose the money is going to be used for and if you plan on paying it back to the policy or not.

In most IUL contracts you can start taking policy loans in year two. Insurance contracts stipulate what percentage of your bucket you can take in loans. Remember, because you are borrowing from the insurance company's general fund and not your bucket of money, the bucket doesn't reduce in size. In other words, you have just collateralized a portion of the value of your bucket (meaning you're using the cash in your bucket as collateral for the loan), but all the money in your bucket is still earning interest, either fixed or indexed depending on how you have the funds allocated.

If you choose the withdrawal-to-basis option, you are reducing your bucket's size by every dollar you withdraw, but sometimes that is the best option. However, there is a pretty stiff stipulation to this. Once the bucket is reduced by using the policy's withdrawal-to-basis option, you can never put the money back into the policy. The bucket has been reduced in size, and it can no longer hold those dollars you withdrew.

Withdrawals permanently reduce the size of your bucket; loans do not reduce the bucket size. Rather, they allow you to return any funds you borrow against your bucket.

Withdrawal-to-basis during the retirement years is the most conservative approach to distributing funds from an Index UL. The fixed or zero spread loan provision will allow tax-free distributions and conserve the size of the death benefit. The Participating loan provision is the more aggressive option. It provides the opportunity to earn a positive spread on the borrowed funds, and this loan also conserves the size of the death benefit. The Fixed Loan or the Participation Loan options allow the owner of the policy to replace the borrowed funds at the owner's discretion, and they do not permanently reduce the death benefit. The Withdrawal to Basis option will permanently reduce the death benefit dollar for dollar, and there is no option to replace the basis—replenish the bucket—in the contract.

If you are retiring, and you are done funding anything, you may want to use your IUL bucket for income purposes. You can use the withdrawal-to-basis option to distribute all your money paid into the policy first, and then borrow against the gains using the zero spread (fixed) loan or the participating loan option. There is a major advantage to this option. Remember how your Social Security gets taxed? Part of the 7702 provision is that the money in your IUL—both the premium and the amount of interest you've earned—is *not* used to means test your income for Social Security or for Medicare. This means if you have income coming out of your IUL policy, this money is not counted against you for reducing your Social Security benefit or increasing your cost of your Medicare Part B. I don't know if you can find anything better for your money in retirement, but that is a decision you have to make for yourself.

Now what if you're not retiring but you want to buy a car or you need to pay for your child's college education—or you have a medical emergency and you don't have enough health insurance to cover it? If you have to (or want to) buy something, you can use the participating loan option in your policy. You have access to the funds all at once but have the option of how you want to pay the loan back—or not. You are using the insurance company's dollars to make a capital purchase, but your money is still inside a compounding growth environment.

Making your Money Work for you Twice

Now what if banks are offering a lower percentage rate on their loans than the insurance company is charging for theirs?

Most of your local banks are willing to collateralize cash inside a life insurance contract for capital purchases. In today's economic environment, the cost to borrow funds from a bank may be cheaper than using the insurance carrier's loan provision. Most banks are charging around 3 to 4 percent for a line of credit that's collateralized by the cash in a life insurance policy. The insurance company, on the other hand, will charge you a 5 to 6 percent loan rate against your policy's cash value. If your money in the Index UL is earning an average of 7 or 8 percent, and you're okay with paying at least the monthly interest on the bank's line of credit, you could do well by using the bank's money at 3 to 4 percent.

If the economic environment changes where the bank's interest rates rise on their line of credit above the insurance carrier's contractual 5 percent rate, you can always borrow the funds from the insurance company and pay off the bank. What if interest rates finally started climbing and the bank comes out with a CD paying 8 percent? Could you go to the insurance company, borrow all the funds you have accumulated in the contract for 5 percent, and put it in a CD making 8 percent? Yes you could. And what if the Index credited 12 percent the next year on your cash in your contract? Would your money be participating in two places earning interest? Yes, it would. You would be earning 8 percent in the CD and earning up to 12 percent in the Index, but it would cost you 5 percent to do all that. I think this is why Albert Einstein thought compounding interest was the eighth wonder of the world.

———◆———

Taking the Plunge

After months and months of research and study, all the elements I had heard about in an Indexed Universal Life policy checked out. I had my three intertwined rings: safety, growth, and income. When I put them together, it formed the shield I wanted for my money from practically the minute I was handed the half-million dollar check for our sign company.

I knew that in an Index Universal Life policy, my nest egg would be protected. I would have money to handle any of life's emergencies that inevitably pop up—and usually at the most inconvenient times. My money would grow so that I could provide for Monica and send my daughter off to a decent college so she could provide for herself. My family was safe because the financial miracle I found really truly delivered what it promised.

To find a local Family Financial Miracle Representative, please visit www.FFMRegistry.com.

7 Shielding Risk

It took me three years from selling my sign company to testing the waters of using a life insurance contract as an alternative savings vehicle. In 2003, I purchased my first Index Universal Life Policy. I started conservatively with $100,000. I needed to see what was going to happen in a real world scenario before I put all of my life savings in one of these contracts. I put in $25,000 a year. I took advantage of another benefit the IUL platform has: getting all the $100,000 in the policy in less than four years. (Depending on your age, you have the option of funding a policy in three years and one day, not five years.) I also chose a product that had a guaranteed 1 percent floor, which means that if the market crashed and went negative in any given year, my account value would still be credited a 1 percent gain. The cap on this IUL policy started out at seventeen percent.

From November 25, 2003 until November 25, 2014, I have made anywhere from $1,069 to $16,015 per year in tax-free interest. And most important, in one of the most vulnerable years in the stock market, I didn't lose a dime. In fact, my account was credited $1,069 in 2008, the one percent guarantee in the contract, which almost covered the entire cost of the $400,000 the insurance company was at risk for insuring me in that year.

It took me four years to get it funded, and I've enjoyed eight years of compounding growth ever since. My money has earned an average of 5.80 percent. I have made $68,789 in interest on my first $100,000. This money is growing in a true compounding environment, and I can draw from this pool of money any time I need it, either through withdrawal-to-basis or by using the policy loan provisions. Either way I can access these funds tax-free.

I bought another IUL policy three years later, on July 26, 2006. I put in an additional $325,000 of my original $450,000. I paid premiums into the contract of $78,000 per year for four years, and $10,000 in the fifth to completely fill the contract to the maximum limit. The death benefit on this second contract is $1.5 million. This policy also has a one percent floor and a fifteen percent cap. Since 2006, this account has averaged a 4.33 percent return, with my total interest earnings at $130,967. I was very happy that I put the rest of our original savings into another IUL policy in 2006 because when the 2008 disaster struck, instead of losing around 40 percent of my account balance, I didn't lose a dime, so my account was able to keep on growing and compounding yearly.

I did a comparison to see what would have happened to my money if I had put it in an equity investment. My original $100,000 would have made a 6.55 percent return. My $325,000 account would have made 6.44 percent over the same time period. Remember, I have been saying that an Indexed Universal Life policy will provide market-*like* returns without market risk.

However, the most telling year is what happened in 2008, the third year I would have made an annual deposit. If I had deposited $78,000 in an equity account that year, I would have lost $91,368. The market loss would have taken away my entire deposit that year along with some of my previous gains. In the IUL, I did not participate in those losses, and I still operate in a true compounding environment.

I know that if my money was in the market right now, I would be enjoying these current high double-digit rates of return, but that means that if the market crashes again, and many indicators point to that happening, perhaps sometime soon, the losses I would sustain would be substantial. As you know, that's a risk I am not willing to take.

You are welcome to view my IUL policy statements at
www.myfamilyfinancialmiracle.com/video.

I also know me. If I had my money in the market, I would be calling my broker every week, "How am I doing?" He would hate it, and so would I, but I would constantly worry about losing my cash.

Shielding Market Risk

It didn't take me long after I learned that my family financial principles were all firmly met in an Index Universal Life policy to decide to get my life insurance license so I could teach others what I had discovered. I believe in the product, and as I told you early on, I wanted others to experience the same benefits as I did with the IUL contracts.

Since 2003, I have helped write hundreds of IUL policies. I have seen the peace of mind that an IUL policy can bring to a family. In fact, everyone I work with will tell you that they are very happy with the product. They often tell me they think I'm clairvoyant because when they get their annual statements, the interests and the costs show them exactly what I had told them from the beginning. They think the policy is not going to work like I say it will.

I have been watching IUL rates of return long enough to know that they are going to average a return of around 6 percent. After a few years, I inevitably get the same phone call: "Wow it's doing what you say." I love it every time because it's an amazing feeling knowing you helped someone. But really there's no magic to it. If you put your money in an environment with no market risk and upside potential that is compounding annually, you're going to show a consistent rate of return. This is only amazing to my clients because of the prevailing ideas about saving money, but once they have been with me long enough to see the consistent returns with the decreasing costs, they are a pretty happy bunch.

Build Cash Faster

Take Jim O. He's getting up into his late eighties, but that doesn't stop him. He's in the Virginia Shagger's Hall of Fame—he's quite the dancer and calls his lady friends "honey." He and I go way back. He knew me when I was running the sign company because he's a builder. Jim is a firm believer in permanent life insurance. He says, "My family has always been of the mind you need to insure yourself and your family because of what might transpire." But, until he met me, he had not been properly enlightened on what an Index Universal Life policy could do. He said his father and others in the family business knew about the protection factor. They all believed it was important to protect their heirs from premature death—no matter when it happened. He had no idea that a permanent life insurance policy could protect his heirs *and* at the same time grow his money.

When I showed Jim how he could build his cash value faster in an Index Universal Life policy, he was amazed. He rolled over his other insurance policies using a 1035 exchange (an IRS provision that allows a policyholder to transfer funds from one policy to another without having to pay taxes) and put all his cash value from his old policies into a new IUL contract. "I was that sure about it," he says. He really enjoyed that he could always put more money into his IUL policy whenever he wanted, and he is quite happy with the returns he's received over the years. "The policy has done exceptionally well. The first year it earned a 10 percent increase. When the recession hit, the returns dropped of course. In the worst year, my policy made 1 percent, but I was happy with that because everyone else was losing money hand over fist. It's averaged way above 6 or 7 percent since."

This is the consistent story I get from people that I have worked with through the crash of 2008. Nelda S. came to me in 2006. She was a referral, and she was tough—my favorite kind of client. I don't think anyone has ever asked me as many questions as she did. Nelda is what's called an "enrolled agent." An enrolled agent is a federally licensed tax practitioner who represents taxpayers before all administrative levels of the Internal Revenue Service. Enrolled agent status is the highest credential awarded by the IRS. Nelda obviously knows her stuff when it comes to taxes. In regards to her own money, she was most interested in using taxes to the best advantage for her family.

She first learned about Index Universal Life when a friend called her asking her what she knew about it. Nelda told her friend, "When something sounds too good to be true, you need to watch out and check it out thoroughly." But Nelda was intrigued herself. Before she went through the rigorous process of becoming an enrolled agent, she worked for the family business keeping the books. She was the one who handled her family's finances.

Nelda, like me, wanted to know everything she could about an IUL contract. "Instead of playing Bridge, I research. If there are rules I can benefit from, I want to know what they are. Especially if I'm looking to retire. I know from experience with my own clients, unless I plan well, I'll be working into my late 70s." She read every reference she could find as well as the tax laws and codes. She literally needed to know all the rules and regulations. She told me, "I was trying to find a hole, but I couldn't find *any*."

As she was signing the IUL contracts for six policies for her and her grandchildren, she said, "I only wish they had been available ten to fifteen years earlier." She continued, "Our savings were in the market. In the late 80s, we got hit hard, and then again in the late 90s and early 2000s. I figured no more." About a year after she bought her policies, the 2008 crash happened. She, like all my clients, was extremely relieved that her money was in a life insurance contract. "If it weren't for our IUL policies, we would have had to dramatically pull back on everything we did in retirement. To live the lifestyle you want, I think you have to pull out of the market."

We talk about why people stay in the market: "People can be greedy. They want to get the highest return on their money as possible. But when the market dips—and it's going to, probably pretty hard—they're going to get hurt. Index Universal Life Insurance gives you a chance to step up, not step back." Nelda has since gotten her life insurance license, and she tells her clients, "I believe they're going to change the 7702 tax code at some point. The wonderful part about it, from a tax standpoint, you get grandfathered. If you purchase an IUL policy for accumulation and protection of your money now, you will not only enjoy peace of mind but be able to take advantage of all the tax benefits it currently offers—tax deferred growth with a way to take tax-free distribution with your heirs receiving the death benefit tax-free. But if you don't get on the bus, you may just miss it." Nelda is obviously very astute about money.

The Tax Shield

Whenever you can take an income distribution on a savings vehicle tax-free, you are in the best type of money environment possible. I have already showed you how tax-free policy loans work, and have discussed when a person may want to take the loan versus using the withdrawal-to basis option.

The IUL policy also offers the benefit of not requiring you to pay tax every year on your interest earnings as you would if your money was in a CD, money market, or equity account.

A husband and wife came to me looking for answers. He was fifty-seven; she was fifty-two. She had just inherited $2 million from her father, and both were very well employed. They didn't need the money. So they dumped half the sum in a bank CD and put the other half with a money manager. No matter the amount, this is the typical way most people manage their money. They have "safe" money earning very little interest and money that is exposed to the high risk of the stock market.

They followed this strategy for a couple of years. She was mainly concerned about the very low returns from her CDs. They were earning less than a point, so she had a million dollars earning very little interest, and if she wanted access to it, she would jeopardize the earnings even more. She also told me the money she had with the money manager was doing well. This was in 2010, when the market was in full recovery from the '08 crash. That's also when the tax problem began to surface. Every year, when she got a 1099 tax statement from her money manager, she paid it out of pocket, like most people do, and went on about her everyday life. The next year, when the 1099 again appeared in her mailbox, she had had enough. That's when she showed up at my office. She said, "All I want for this inheritance is to earn a decent rate of return on it without being taxed to death, so I have something to pass onto my children and grandchildren."

I asked her how much was she paying in taxes annually. She told me $10,000 to $15,000 a year. I then asked her how she was paying it. She shrugged and said, "I just pay the tax." In other words, she had no tax-saving strategy at all, and let me tell you, this is a savvy woman when it comes to money and handling finances. Yet she had seen no other way out of her tax mess than to pay Uncle Sam out of her ordinary income.

I asked, "Why don't you get the money to pay your taxes out of your mutual funds?"

She rolled her eyes, sighed, and said, "Because it's too much trouble to go into the account, sell the stock and do all the paperwork just to pay off the $10,000 or $15,000." Then her eyes narrowed: "The other problem is that if the market is down that day, then we would sell the stock at a discount. We'd be losing money to pay money to cover the tax on the money we're trying to protect! We figured we're better off leaving it all in there, let it ride, and just write the check."

When I looked at her $10,000 to $15,000 tax statements, I knew those numbers were conservative at best. Here's the real problem: In a good year, let's say she makes a 10 percent return on her managed money, or $100,000. Because she's in a 30 percent-plus tax bracket, she would have to foot the bill for $30,000 in taxes that year. She knew that, too.

I asked her, "What if I could show you a way you can keep all of that tax money?"

She was all ears. She told me her inheritance was quickly becoming a burden because she worried too much about her money, and she had to pay that nasty tax bill every year out of her and her husband's "lifestyle" money—money they used for vacations and entertainment.

When I showed her how an IUL policy holds up to the three family financial principles of growth, protection, and income through liquidity, use, and control, and has the all-important death benefit added for her legacy, she agreed that was the best place for her money. She said that she wished she would have known about this alternative in the first place; she would have saved $25,000 in taxes!

Then I showed her how her money would grow over the years. Her $1 million Guideline Single Premium, broken into five payments over five years, would give her a death benefit of $2.7 million. That immediately created another $1.7 million in assets for her heirs—because, remember, the one million she put in becomes part of the death benefit. Today, the cash is sitting there compounding into a mountain of wealth. Over time, that initial $1million premium will drive up the value of the policy because the death benefit increases in direct ratio to the increasing cash value caused by the annual interest earned. By her eighty-fifth birthday, that $1 million of inheritance money will grow to around $6 million, earnings on which she could have zero tax liability. The policy Death Benefit will be worth $6.3 million—tax-free to her heirs.

When it is used properly, the Index Universal Life policy is one of the most effective tools used in legacy planning today. When she came to me, this woman wanted to make sure that the original $2 million would be her legacy. Now, her $2 million is more than covered by the IUL policy, which leaves the other $1 million in the CDs free for her and her husband to enjoy as they wish.

Qualified Money

While not everyone is going to have a $2 million inheritance to play with, many of my clients have savings, sometimes substantial, in 401(k)s and IRAs. They come to me in their late thirties to mid-forties, and they tend to be in the higher wage brackets with annual incomes of at least $100,000. Sometimes their income is less, and that's fine.

One of my clients is a doctor who makes about $250,000 a year. His wife is a stay-at-home mom with their four children. (So imagine how much she's really worth!) He had $50,000 of their annual savings going into his company's deferred compensation plan. When we met in 2013, his account balance was $500,000. The account had just made up the losses the doctor had suffered in 2008 and was up just a little. He finally had suffered enough market loss in his government qualified, deferred compensation plan. In other words, he was definitely market adverse, and he also knew that he would eventually be exposed to some pretty hefty tax liabilities with his amount of savings.

He'd been opposed to life insurance options because an advisor of some kind had used antiquated information to convince him that *all* life insurance is the same, that all life insurance products are expensive with no potential to create wealth. He, like many others, bought term life insurance to protect his family from his premature death, and invested his savings in his qualified retirement plan.

I showed him an illustration of what could happen to his money if he used the same $50,000 he was putting into his qualified plan into an IUL policy. First, he would need to pay a 28 percent income tax on the $50,000 since the government does not allow premiums to go into a permanent life insurance contract pre-taxed. That would leave him $36,000 to fund an IUL policy.

When the doctor saw the illustrations and comparison to a qualified plan, he was truly amazed. If he continued to put in $50,000 a year into his qualified plan by age sixty-five, he would have a total of $2,172,569 taxable dollars. I ran the projections using an average 8 percent return. I picked age sixty-six because that is typically when people start taking distributions. Of course, this figure would be less if the market crashed. If he put $36,000 every year into the IUL, he would amass $1,422,278 tax-free, by the age of sixty six with a death benefit of $2,181,208. That's a $750,291 dollar difference between the qualified plan and the IUL contract, but the difference comes to around 35 percent, or most likely the amount of taxes due to the IRS on distribution of the qualified funds.

Then I showed him what would happen to his money over a twenty-six year period from sixty-six to ninety, taking an income of $154,146 per year from the IUL policy using a tax-free policy loan. At age ninety, his life expectancy, he will have taken a total of $3,699,504, and he still would have a $1,000,064 death benefit for his heirs. If he lives longer than ninety, he still would be able to take his annual distribution. Here is the table that shows you the annual numbers:

Universal Life Contract Illustration

Year	Age	Ann Prem	Income	Acc Val	Surrender	Death Ben	Internal ROR
1	46	$36,000		$32,356	$ 10,294	$791,286	-71.41%
2	47	$36,000		$67,004	$ 47,143	$825,934	-25.12%
3	48	$36,000		$104,138	$ 86,486	$863,068	-10.70%
4	49	$36,000		$143,970	$ 128,525	$902,900	-4.50%
5	50	$36,000		$186,676	$ 173,441	$945,606	-1.23%
19	64	$36,000		$1,292,817	$ 1,292,817	$2,051,747	6.03%
20	65	$36,000		$1,422,278	$ 1,422,278	$2,181,208	6.11%
21	66	$0	$154,146	$1,526,012	$ 1,364,159	$1,669,361	6.21%
22	67	$0	$154,146	$1,637,194	$ 1,305,394	$1,616,461	6.30%
23	68	$0	$154,146	$1,756,366	$ 1,246,123	$1,562,269	6.39%
24	69	$0	$154,146	$1,884,113	$ 1,186,505	$1,506,804	6.48%
38	83	$0	$154,146	$5,101,146	$ 547,827	$802,884	7.75%
39	84	$0	$154,146	$5,474,817	$ 531,979	$805,719	7.83%
40	85	$0	$154,146	$5,874,522	$ 522,688	$816,414	7.90%
41	86	$0	$154,146	$6,301,618	$ 520,339	$835,420	7.98%
42	87	$0	$154,146	$6,757,391	$ 525,195	$863,064	8.04%
43	88	$0	$154,146	$7,243,149	$ 537,490	$899,647	8.11%
44	89	$0	$154,146	$7,760,145	$ 557,349	$945,356	8.17%
45	90	$0	$154,146	$8,309,383	$ 584,595	$1,000,064	8.23%

However, the qualified plan money showed a very different scenario. Even though he started out at age sixty-six with $750,291 more in the qualified plan, his money wouldn't last as long taking the same spendable amount of distribution. Here's how that works. If he wants to match the $154,146 yearly income, he would have to withdraw $192,758 a year so he could cover his tax bill, if his effective income tax rate is 20 percent. He would have to pay more if taxes increase. By the time he turns eighty-five, his account has zeroed out—and that's the good news in this scenario. If the market dips, or worse crashes, in those twenty years he's taking distributions, then he's in a very poor "sequence of returns" situation in which he's taking distributions and losing money in the market but is no longer making annual deposits to offset the losses. In this scenario his account will be depleted even sooner.

Here is the chart that shows how this works. He deposits $50,000 annually into his tax-deferred qualified plan. It earns the 8 percent average interest a year. He starts taking distribution at age sixty-six, and the account is depleted, completely, by age eighty-five.

Qualified Plan Illustration

Year	Age	Deposit	Gross w/d	Mgmt fees	Interest	EOY total
1	46	$50,000		$540	$ 400	$53,460
2	47	$50,000		$1,117	$ 8,277	$110,619
3	48	$50,000		$1,735	$ 12,850	$171,734
4	49	$50,000		$2,395	$ 17,739	$237,078
5	50	$50,000		$3,100	$ 22,966	$306,944
19	64	$50,000		$20,020	$ 148,295	$1,981,958
20	65	$50,000		$21,945	$ 162,557	$2,172,569
21	66		$192,758	$21,382	$ 158,385	$2,116,814
22	67		$192,758	$20,780	$ 153,924	$2,057,200
23	68		$192,758	$20,136	$ 149,155	$1,993,461
24	69		$192,758	$19,448	$ 144,056	$1,925,311
37	82		$192,758	$4,700	$ 34,818	$465,337
38	83		$192,758	$2,944	$ 21,806	$291,441
39	84		$192,758	$1,066	$ 7,895	$105,511
40	85		$105,511	$0	$ -	$0
41	86		$0	$0	$ -	$0
42	87		$0	$0	$ -	$0
43	88		$0	$0	$ -	$0

The doctor agreed he'd be much better off in an IUL contract. By handling his annual savings this way, he saw how he eliminated the market risk he had become so adverse to. The future tax risk he was so worried about was gone. This was especially important because given his profession, his annual income was never guaranteed. I also reminded him that having his savings in an IUL policy also freed up his retirement savings from government restrictions and penalties if he wanted to access the funds for other future ventures prior to him turning 59 ½.

For an in-depth explanation of how an IUL protects you from running out of money in your retirement, please visit www.myfamilyfinancialmiracle.com/video.

That's when the doctor groaned. I asked him what was going on. He told me that just a year prior to our meeting, his brother came up with a remarkable investment opportunity. A friend of his had discovered oil on his land and needed money for his oil-drilling operation. Geologists said the well was certain to produce a profit. Investors who put up $100,000 for drilling would share in the "mother lode." Because all of the doctor's savings was locked up in his qualified plan, he didn't have free access to his retirement money without paying the penalty and tax liability. This equaled roughly 49 percent if you figure 10 percent penalty, 33 percent federal tax and around 6 percent state tax. In essence, if he took his money out, he'd be getting fifty cents on the dollar. If he put that money into the oil well, he would assume the new risk on that investment. He wasn't willing to take that big of a hit on his savings and take on the new risk too. His brother and other partners more than doubled their money on the drilling operation. Lack of liquidity kept the doctor from an incredible investment opportunity.

Had the doctor put his money in an IUL, he could have collateralized the cash in his policy to invest in the drilling operation by using a policy loan. Remember, in a policy loan, he's not touching his money; he would be using the insurance company's money from their general account, which would charge him 5 percent interest. Now let's also say that the market did very well that year, maybe 20 percent, and his index cap was 15 percent. His cash value is still earning 15 percent; he's paying 5 percent for the loan. There's a huge difference between paying 5 percent and 49 percent to get access to your money.

Once the doctor understood how flexible an IUL policy really is and that he could earn interest on his money while it's in the policy and also use the collateralized cash in any investment he chose, he could see the possibilities. What if he wanted to buy bargain-priced real estate? If his money is tied up in IRA-bound mutual funds, he wouldn't be able to access the money in time to satisfy the purchase contract.

Whatever it is that you want to buy or invest in becomes possible with an IUL policy loan. In chapter 6, I talked about the possibility of buying a CD at 8 percent with collateralized cash from a policy loan if the interest rates ever returned to the highs of the early 1990s. Whether it is real estate, market investing, or other ways to grow your money, if you have an IUL policy, you can have your money do two things at once with the policy loan, and you're still earning interest on your money.

As the doctor started planning out how he was going to invest more of his money, I told him he had to keep one thing in mind. When you are taking loans on your policy, you have to deal with something called collateral capacity. That is the difference between the amount of money you already have collateralized and the amount you can collateralize in future loans.

If you have $100,000 in cash value in your policy, and you borrow $50,000, you cannot borrow against the money you already have collateralized. Insurance companies do have guidelines on the percentage of your cash value that can be loaned, and each company is different. Most of the policies that I write for my clients have a very high percentage, even as high as 90 percent. If that limit is 90 percent, or $90,000, and you have already borrowed $50,000, you have the collateral capacity to borrow another $40,000 against the value of this policy. If you don't pay it back, you have used up all of your collateral capacity. If you do pay it back, then the collateral capacity is available again. You can use your collateral capacity to invest in other things. You pay it back, you have it there to use once again. If you choose not to pay the policy loan back, the amount you borrowed will be deducted from your death benefit that goes to your heirs because the death benefit covers the collateral. However, if the distribution is set up correctly, you don't have to worry about outliving your money.

If a person decides they do not want their savings in a qualified plan, I have helped him or her strategically roll that money out into an IUL policy. This is normally done after the client turns 59 ½ so there's no penalty. We roll it out in such a way to minimize the tax liability every year until all the money is moved over. All my clients who have made the switch are glad they did. They see the consistent rates of return. They get rid of future tax liability. They have the upside potential of the market without market losses, the tax-free loans—all the benefits the IUL provides once they get the policy funded.

How Living Benefits Handle Life Risks

With an IUL, you have created your own private reserve of money from which you can collateralize using a policy loan to help fund anything from a car to your child's college education. Because your money is protected, it is earning a consistent rate of return, and you can use it whatever way you want.

When I showed my client, the heiress, how she could save money on taxes plus enjoy all the tax-advantaged solutions an IUL contract offers, she called it a "miracle." That's when I began to refer to what I had learned as "My Family Financial Miracle." I had developed effective strategies to be able to take advantage of all the living benefits an IUL policy offered. I had counseled hundreds of people on how they could finance their own capital purchases like cars or even down payments for houses. Forget 529 college savings plans. Buy an IUL policy for your child when he or she is young. Fund it at $200 to $300 a month. When it comes time for them to leave the nest, they won't have to take out student loans. They could take a loan against their very own IUL policy, and they wouldn't be paying back a bank or a government-run loan service. They would be paying back the insurance company on a non-structured loan. They could choose to free up the collateral capacity or they could just max it out. It's up to them. Out of that pool of money, however, they could then finance their own cars, the down payment for their first home—the list is endless.

While both my clients and I get excited about all the possibilities, I remind them that it's how an IUL policy can truly help mitigate the life risks I talked about in chapter 4 that's important. To recap, they are catastrophic illness; long-term care; job loss; the problem of longevity or outliving your retirement; legal action; premature death, and inflation.

The first level of protection is really the death benefit in case of premature death. Next is the guarantee on your hard-earned principal. Then it just keeps getting better. The caps and the floors keep you in the middle of the road, or as my granddad would say, "keep 'em between the ditches." The lock-in and reset of the index every year is huge, and actually gives you a reason to celebrate a poor performing market when it occurs because you know the next year the market will perform well and you will most likely earn your full cap in interest in the index allocation.

The access to the cash tax-free through policy loans is genius. The government doesn't tax IUL policy loans. You can take a loan against the policy anytime there is cash in the policy, but remember the money is not taken out of your policy. Your cash value stays in your policy allocated as you have set it up; the borrowed funds come from the insurance company's general account. That means your cash is still in the policy earning compounding interest every year.

There are other layers of protection most permanent life insurance policies handle. They're called "riders." You may have heard of them. They can actually pay your scheduled annual premiums; they can handle long-term care expenses; they can do many things and offer you an even greater amount of flexibility of protection. They do come at a cost, however, and because they are somewhat complicated, I'm going to save an in-depth look at riders for another time. For now, know that your tax-free loan or withdrawal-to-basis options can handle the life risks that will happen to all of us at some point in our lives. Let's take a look to see what can be done:

Catastrophic illness: the technical definition of catastrophic illness means you have contracted some kind of fatal illness or suffered a fatal injury, and your life expectancy is low, around six months to a year. Permanent life insurance has a provision for this called the accelerated death benefit. This means that you can contact the insurance company, show them proof that you have a catastrophic illness, and you would have access up to half of your death benefit while you are still alive. It will cost you a certain percentage, but you will have your money, tax-free, to use as you see fit.

Long-term care costs can be handled with a policy loan. Remember the man who had the heart problem and couldn't work for a year and a half? If he had funded an IUL, he could take a tax-free policy loan to cover his expenses. He could then choose to pay it back when he was able to work so his death benefit would stay intact. If he chose not to pay it back, the death benefit would be affected when he passed away.

Job loss works the same way. If you lose your job or are transferred and take a pay cut, having access to the cash in your IUL through a policy loan can handle the interrupted cash flow. Once you go back to work, you can replenish the policy's collateral capacity by systematically paying off the borrowed funds. Remember your policy's cash value didn't go anywhere; it is still earning compounded interest in an index allocation. You haven't lost your savings in the job transfer.

Longevity: I have already covered this in the doctor's example. However, it is important to underscore the point that an IUL potentially alleviates the risk of you outliving your savings. For baby boomers, this risk is probably the uppermost on their minds. There has been a shift in thinking recently. As baby boomers leave the work force, they are becoming more concerned with income distribution from their savings as opposed to wealth accumulation.

An IUL policy offers a hedge against managing retirement income. Because the loan distributions from an IUL are not taxed, you know exactly how much you need to distribute to net a certain amount of money. There is no more guesswork trying to estimate the net spendable dollar you have available from a retirement account distribution. If funded properly during your earning years, then during your retirements years, these contracts can be optimized for cost and risk. There's no market risk, no tax risk, and the cost per year is as low as any savings vehicle where you store money and earn a rate of return.

Also, as I have mentioned before, when you take out an IUL policy loan, your Social Security is not affected. Because it is a loan, it is not considered part of the means testing the Social Security administration requires. However, your policy is considered for a Medicaid spend down, and if you do need to use it for that purpose, you can use the withdrawal-to-basis option to access the money. By using an IUL during this time, your tax consequences would not be as high as if you had to take money out of an IRA.

When it comes to *legal action,* your money in a permanent life insurance policy is protected from legal settlements in most states. If you suffer the tragedy of a lawsuit, the settlement cannot include the funds inside your IUL policy.

Premature death is of course covered in the death benefit. But that death benefit can also help pay for the costs of your loved-one's funeral without it compromising your ability to continue to pay your bills as you work through the grieving process and move forward with life.

As for *inflation,* let me have Nelda explain how she looks at an IUL policy. She calls her policies her "inflation protection." She's pretty emphatic: "It's the only product out there in which you don't go backwards. You're protected. This is important in retirement. When you're working, if you have a bad year in your 401(k), it's called a 'paper loss.' You're still putting money into your account so you don't feel the hit as much. When you retire, you don't have a way to make up those losses in the same manner. I wasn't willing to do that with our retirement." I suggest to my clients to use their qualified money during the early years of retirement. This way they are spending all the taxable money first, leaving the tax-free money in their IUL to continue to compound. It also is in the best interest of their heirs. It is always better to pass on to the next generation tax-free money versus taxable money. When you get to your later retirement years, and you have exhausted all your taxable and tax-deferred accounts, you have an IUL policy that is still growing and you can use to support yourself and your spouse.

For me, an Index Universal Life policy isn't just about the money. It's what I have been talking about all along—the peace of mind knowing your money is protected. It's shielded from loss and from taxes. It can give you much needed cash flow when other options are either not available or have run out.

I once had a man come into my office. He was ecstatic because he had just sold a house that he had purchased for $100,000 for $400,000. He told me that house, which was an investment property, was the "best investment he's ever made." This was before the housing bubble burst in '08.

He was heading into his retirement years, however, and he wanted a place where he could park his earnings. I asked him how long he had owned his home: twenty years. I figured it up and his return was 7 percent. However, he had to pay capital gains tax on the money he made from the sale. At 20 percent that's $60,000 out of his pocket. That reduced the amount of his return to 6.30 percent. I asked him, "Did you ever worry that the house would lose value?" He said he had thought about it, but the housing market was so strong he didn't really lose any sleep over it. After I showed him all the benefits an Index Universal Life policy had to offer, he bought a policy using a large portion of his $340,000. I told him, "If the greatest investment you ever made created a 6 percent return, you're going to be really happy with the IUL."

After the housing bubble burst he called me. "I know permanent life insurance is not an investment. But I would have lost at least one third of the value of that house had I not sold it when I did. I thank the heavens above that I got out when I did and you showed me the value of life insurance. *That* is the greatest peace-of-mind investment I have definitely ever made."

I will take calls like that all day long. I wish for you the same peace of mind that my clients have been enjoying for the past fifteen years.

To find a local Family Financial Miracle Representative, please visit www.FFMRegistry.com.

8 Untruths and Misconceptions

As I was researching Index Universal Life policies, I had run into various odd ideas about them. Once I became an agent and started talking to others, I found there are some major misconceptions out there about life insurance.

Because the finance experts on TV say "life insurance is too expensive," you believe it. But here's the problem. The TV experts are not life insurance experts and spend most of their time studying the stock market and real estate investing. That's fine, but they really don't understand how Index Universal life insurance works, and how its costs can *decrease* the longer you own it. If they really looked at how you can optimize earnings in an environment that is extremely safe—even safer than banks—they may change the way they think.

As I said in the previous chapter, I like it most when I'm in control of my money. I'm not alone in this. I met one of my clients when he was thirty-two years old. He owned a very successful business putting expensive sound systems into people's homes. He came to one of my seminars because he had $500,000 in savings. He told me, "I've got a lot of money, but I'm not going to waste it. I don't need to make huge returns. I just want something that can provide safe and consistent earnings." He made a point to tell me that while the prevailing idea was that he should be able to afford to take risks in the open market because he was so young, he said, "I would rather get a consistent 5 percent rate of return every year. Time is in my favor in a real compounding environment. I would like to make market-like returns, but I have to be able to sleep at night."

So he asked me how much insurance $500,000 worth of premium would buy. I told him his death benefit would have to be $3.5 million. He didn't flinch. We set up his policy to fund over five years, as per the IRS 7702 rules. The policy is over ten years old and the cash value is almost a million dollars. Does he need a $3.5 million death benefit? Maybe. Maybe not. What he's getting, however, is some pretty sound sleep at night. What's the value of that? To some, it's priceless.

Benefits Cost

The death benefit, I have already told you, is the reason why life insurance exists. Without it, you would be in the realm of investments which is governed by SEC regulations—a realm that I don't deal in.

The death benefit is why people think of life insurance as "death insurance." Life insurance does provide a way to give your heirs a financial legacy—income-tax free no less—that can't be rivaled anywhere. As I said to my builder, why knock something that comes along for the ride anyway? But life insurance really is for the living. Optimizing the cash value in a permanent life insurance policy through true compounding and then accessing it through policy loans, tax-free, are the "living benefits" of the product.

The two together—the living benefits and death benefit—work in relation with one another throughout the entire life of the policy. When you understand how to optimize that relationship, you can dispel the myth that life insurance policies get more expensive the older we get or the longer we own them. Here's the key: when a life insurance policy is properly designed for cash accumulation, its value increases over time which actually decreases the cost.

Life Insurance Costs Outlined

Every financial product that is available to hold and grow money has a cost. From savings accounts to equity investments, I don't know of any financial product you can save and grow money in that doesn't. The cost of the death benefit is called the mortality cost; it is the net amount that is at risk for the insurance company to pay to an heir. The mortality cost is what you're paying for in a life insurance policy.

Our responsibility as good stewards of our money is to minimize, or control cost, while protecting and growing our money without ever interrupting the compounding process. To control any cost, you have to know what it is and how it works.

To support all the benefits in a policy, there are four charges in a permanent life insurance policy: the premium charge, the policy fee, the unit charge, and the cost of insurance.

- The premium charge is also called the load. It's the cost to the buyer for putting the premium into the policy. It is only charged against the annual premiums. Once the premium is fully paid, then no more premium charges. These "loads" are used to cover the taxes the state charges the insurance company to do business in that state.

- The policy fee is the administrative costs. It is charged every year for the life of the policy.

- The unit charge is a flat or static fee all insurance companies charge. It is an expense charge per each thousand dollars of the face (the death benefit). So if you have a $300,000 face, then the unit cost is going to be figured on each thousand dollars of the three hundred. Insurance companies have different "per thousand fee" charges, but they all charge it. Normally, it is charged for the first ten years of the policy, and it doesn't matter if you max fund the policy sooner or not. It is a charge that is balanced against the cost of insurance.

- The cost of insurance, or COI, is how much the insurance carrier is charging you to cover the death benefit. I have mentioned the cost of insurance throughout the book, and it is perhaps the most misunderstood charge of the four. No matter when you die, the insurance company must pay the death benefit specified in the life contract. How much the insurance company is on the hook to pay to the beneficiary depends upon how much cash value is in the policy at the time of death. The closer your cash value is to the value of the death benefit, the less you are charged each year for the mortality. If your death benefit is $300,000 and you have accumulated $150,000 in cash value in your policy, you are only being charged the mortality cost for $150,000 of life insurance that year. Why? The insurance company has to pay the net amount at risk, the $150,000 difference. In other words, the difference between the contracted death benefit and the cash value is what you are being charged for. Thus, if the policy is structured correctly, the amount of insurance you are having to purchase reduces each year as the cash value increases.

When you structure your policy to maximize the growth of your cash, your cash value is there to be used for your living benefits, as well as to pay the death benefit to your beneficiary according to IRS codes, federal law, and the insurance company's policy. You can structure a life policy to pay the death benefit in addition to your cash accumulated value to your heir, but that increases the annual cost of the insurance instead of decreasing it. You would choose this option only if you were buying the policy solely for the death benefit.

Is it right that the insurance company considered your cash value part of the death benefit? Yes, especially when you consider this option is what allows you to be able to compound the cash inside the Index UL policy each year. The more cash you have in the contract, the less the contract costs to own; the less the contract costs to own, the more gains there are to participate in the next year's earnings.

The cost of insurance is always there. It is more expensive in the beginning years of the policy because that is when your cash value is at its lowest and thus you are being charged close to the entire death benefit. The annual cost of insurance will be reduced by increasing the amount of cash value you have in your policy. Cash value increases in two ways: by you putting the premiums in the policy as quickly as you are legally allowed to, and by the policy being credited interest from the two crediting options (fixed or indexed) you chose the cash to participate in.

To show you how this works, here's an example of an Index Universal Life policy for a forty-five year old female with a death benefit of $500,000 when the contract is fully funded. It was funded over the course of fifteen years at $12,000 per year, and it shows the various costs over a twenty-year period:

Index Universal Life Policy Charges and Expense Detail

Year	Age	Plan Prem	Prem Chg	Pol Fee	Unit Chg	COI	Total
1	46	$12,000	$600	$90	$1,226	$450	$2,366
2	47	$12,000	$600	$90	$1,226	$492	$2,409
3	48	$12,000	$600	$90	$1,226	$527	$2,444
4	49	$12,000	$600	$90	$1,226	$555	$2,471
5	50	$12,000	$600	$90	$1,226	$590	$2,506
6	51	$12,000	$600	$90	$1,226	$563	$2,479
7	52	$12,000	$600	$90	$1,226	$537	$2,453
8	53	$12,000	$600	$90	$1,226	$505	$2,421
9	54	$12,000	$600	$90	$1,226	$463	$2,379
10	55	$12,000	$600	$90	$1,226	$408	$2,325
11	56	$12,000	$600	$90	$0	$456	$1,146
12	57	$12,000	$600	$90	$0	$513	$1,203
13	58	$12,000	$600	$90	$0	$579	$1,269
14	59	$12,000	$600	$90	$0	$655	$1,345
15	60	$12,000	$600	$90	$0	$739	$1,429
16	61	$0	$0	$90	$0	$431	$521
17	62	$0	$0	$90	$0	$481	$571
18	63	$0	$0	$90	$0	$538	$628
19	64	$0	$0	$90	$0	$597	$687
20	65	$0	$0	$90	$0	$656	$746
TOT		$180,000	$9,000	$1,800	$12,260	$10,735	$33,798

5%

Notice how these various charges work:

- Through year fifteen, the policy owner is charged $600 per year for each year the premium is deposited. In year sixteen, the premium charge ends because the contract is fully funded.

- The policy fee is very low—$90 a year. It's the annual fee that lasts the life of the contract.

- The unit charge of $1,226 is done in year ten as is the norm.

- The cost of insurance (which is the cost of mortality), starts at $450 and increases to $739 in year fifteen, then drops to $431 in year sixteen. That has to do with the way the death benefit was built for this policy. The death benefit started out at $270,000, and it increased to $530,000 over the fifteen years. In year sixteen the death benefit was dropped by the owner of the policy to $380,000. The cost dropped from $739 to $431 that year. All of these changes in the policy are done internally by the carrier for no additional charge, and the policy stays in compliance with the IRS rules. In year sixteen there is $300,000 cash in this policy. The total cost that year to manage and provide the death benefit is $431. If you were to earn 10 percent on this $300,000 in a taxable asset you would pay a minimum of 15 percent in taxes on the gain of the $30,000 or $4,500 in income taxes. Think about this: the money you save by not having to pay the *annual* taxes on the gains in this contract—if the money was in an equity account—is sufficient to cover *all* the previous years plus any future year's cost of this contract.

Now, notice something about the total cost—all four categories of cost added together. From year one through year ten, the total annual cost goes from $2,366 to $2,325, hardly any difference, but in year eleven, the unit charge drops off. You're no longer being charged the $1,226 a year.

In the next section of this chapter, I am going to show you a hypothetical equity account so you can compare how much you're paying in fees and taxes on the same $12,000 annual deposit. For now, remember the value of a permanent life insurance policy—all the living benefits you receive—and ask yourself if you are getting your money's worth. You have a savings vehicle in which your money is protected; it is growing with market-like returns but in a true compounding environment; you have access to your money tax-free through policy loans; should you die prematurely, your beneficiaries receive the death benefit tax-free.

In the example we're looking at, over the course of fifteen years, the woman has paid for all those benefits, but because her money is growing steadily, with no loss, the cash value of her policy is building, which is ultimately going to decrease her insurance costs the longer she holds the policy.

> To view another demonstration on Cost of Insurance, please visit www.myfamilyfinancialmiracle.com/video.

Age Matters

The cost of insurance is higher in the beginning years of a life contract because of the net amount of risk the insurance carrier is on the hook to pay. This is important to really understand because once the policy has been issued, the insurance company is required to pay the death benefit of the policy should the person insured die unexpectedly, even on the day of the policy being issued.

But here's where things can get confusing. The mortality cost increases with age.

"But wait," you say, "you just said that the cost of insurance reduces the longer you own a policy." If mortality cost is increasing yearly with age (thus fueling the myth that life insurance policies get more expensive the older we get), how can the cost of insurance be reduced with age?

First, let me use a golf tournament analogy to explain why age matters: everyone is familiar with a hole in one. In golf tournaments, there's usually a hole-in-one contest that you pay $10 or so to enter. The payout is usually pretty substantial, say $100,000. The risk to the tournament producers that someone is going to hit that hole in one is pretty low if the tee is a couple hundred yards away from the hole. However, the risk of someone hitting a hole in one increases the closer the golfer gets to the hole. If you were only three yards away from the hole, then you would expect to pay a lot more than $10 to participate for a $100,000 prize. In the world of life insurance, the younger a person is, the less chance he or she has of dying. So that means less risk to the insurance company so less cost per thousand dollars of mortality, or "per thousand." The older a person is the more risk the insurance company takes on. The more risk there is the more the insurance costs per thousand.

Mortality or actuary tables, the tables insurance companies use to figure the cost of the insurance, show the statistical probability of a person dying before their next birthday based on their age. This is how insurance companies figure the "per thousand" cost of the insurance. The older you are, obviously the higher the statistical chance you have of passing away. That means the insurance company is at a higher risk to pay the death benefit should you die. So the cost of insurance per thousand dollars increases as you get older. However, this cost is offset the longer you own your policy because the more money and interest you accumulate, the less amount of insurance you have to pay for.

This is how it works. Let's say you're fifty years old and the total amount of premium you want to put into the contract (the GSP) is $100,000. The minimum corresponding death benefit to a $100,000 premium for the policy you're looking at is $360,000. That latter amount will qualify the contract as an Index Universal Life policy, as long as the $100,000 is put into the policy no quicker than over a five year period. The insurance company's risk is at its highest during those first five years because it would have to cover almost the entire $360,000 death benefit should you die.

You take five years to put in the total premium of $100,000. In year five, the amount the insurance company would have to pay is $260,000: $360,000 minus $100,000. So in year five, when the policy is max funded, the cost of insurance, or the amount on which the mortality cost is figured, will be calculated on $260,000 for a fifty-year old. This is why the mortality cost is a net amount—it's the death benefit minus the cash value. In year one, that cost is $657.

Fast forward ten years; the cash value is $160,000, the death benefit is still $360,000, and you're now sixty years old. The difference is $200,000. If you died unexpectedly, the insurance company would have to pay your beneficiaries $200,000 and the remaining $160,000 would come from the cash in your policy. The cost for that year for the mortality is $685—not a lot of difference from year one through five.

Add ten more years; you're now seventy years old. The $100,000 is now worth $340,000, and the death benefit is $390,000. The death benefit increased by $30,000. The reason for that is a certain differential between the cash value and the death benefit must be maintained for the contract to keep its status as permanent life insurance. This differential is dictated by IRS code 7702. When you have a death benefit of $390,000 and a cash value of $340,000, how much insurance are you purchasing? $50,000. The mortality cost on that amount of insurance at age seventy years old is $469, over two hundred dollars less per year than when you were sixty.

The cost of the insurance does not go down because you are older; rather it decreases because the cash value of the policy has increased. Thus, the difference between the cash value you have in your policy and the amount of death benefit the insurance company has to pay is much less.

This is why max funded Index Universal life contracts cost less the longer you own them, and this is why the IUL is an excellent retirement saving alternative; during the time you need the money the most, the cost to own the product is less.

The Corridor

There is actually a name for the differential, the balancing act between the cash value and the death benefit. It's called the corridor, and insurance companies continually monitor this in your policy.

Above I said that the ideal scene in a permanent life insurance policy is when you can control the costs of the insurance while optimizing your earnings. The corridor—the difference between the cash value and the death benefit—shows you how that is done.

This graph shows the corridor in the same life insurance policy I talked about above—the forty-five year old female depositing a $12,000 premium a year for fifteen years. The dashed line is the cash value; the solid line is the death benefit.

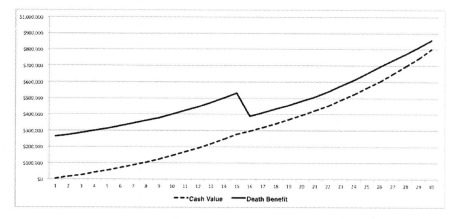

For the first fifteen years, there is a steady but wide gap between the cash value and the death benefit. Then in year sixteen, the same year the cost of insurance reduces from $739 to $431 (from the chart on page 105), the policy reduces the amount of the death benefit. When the amount of death benefit gets closer to matching the cash value in the policy, the distance between the two lines narrows considerably. That space, whether it is wide or narrow, is the corridor.

The corridor must be present in order for the contract to be classified as an Index Universal Life policy, but as your age increases, the spread in the corridor decreases if the policy is funded correctly. When you turn ninety-five, the corridor collapses—there is no difference between the cash value and the death benefit. However, if the corridor collapsed while the contract is being funded, including putting in the entire premium (the GSP) all at once, then you would be in a MEC environment and you would lose the tax advantages of the Index UL policy.

Here is the crux to the entire puzzle of making an Index Universal Life contract work for cash accumulation: controlling the cost in an IUL contract is done by narrowing the corridor—closing the gap between the cash value of the policy and the death benefit as quickly as you possibly can while keeping in line with the IRS guidelines 7702. This is the maximum efficiency I have mentioned before.

Why is the policy so efficient? Because the difference between the cash in the policy and the death benefit the insurance company is on the hook to pay to your beneficiary is very small, so the cost of insurance is very low. This leaves more money in the policy earning interest.

Take another look at the line graph above. When the cash value is $313,000, the death benefit is $407,000. The difference, $94,000, is the death benefit the insurance company is at risk to pay above the cash value. So the policy owner pays insurance on the $94,000 not $407,000.

To reach maximum efficiency, you want to fund the policy as fast as you are able with the maximum amount of premium that you can in order to have the internal cost of the policy be as low as possible. This is the importance of the 7-pay test with the added benefit of the IUL being able to be fully funded in five years.

Think about what would happen if this same policy was funded in five years. The Guideline Single Premium is $180,000. Divide that by five and you get $36,000. You put $36,000 a year into the policy for five years, what is going to happen?

- The premium charge will go away in year six.
- The cost of insurance decreases because the amount of the cash in the policy increases
- The amount of money in the policy is more per year, so it is making more interest and the compounding environment increases.

That is controlling the cost while maximizing the benefits.

The Death Benefit Increase

There is one more element to an Index Universal Life Insurance policy that works to your advantage, and it again has to do with the corridor and how you structure the death benefit. There are a number of different options you can choose for the death benefit. I noted above that you can choose to build a policy where the cash value plus the original death benefit is paid to your heirs, but that's a policy built primarily for legacy purposes.

To optimize the cash value, you have two choices. You can start with a level death benefit. That is ideal if you can fully fund the policy in the shortest amount of time. However, the policy owner we've been studying knew she couldn't fund the policy fully in five years, so she chose the option that allows the death benefit to start out low and to increase yearly as the cash value increases. She knew that if she started out with a $500,000 death benefit, the corridor would have been too wide for too long a period of time; the cost of insurance would have been correspondingly prohibitive in the early years. She would have had to pay the difference between her premium of $12,000 and the death benefit of $500,000 each year, which would probably double or triple her annual cost of the mortality. This would have cut into the amount of interest she could potentially earn on her accumulated cash.

Since she knew that the best way to grow cash is by keeping a minimum distance between the cash value and the death benefit, she chose the option of having the death benefit increase over time. So, if you look at the next chart, you will see that as the premiums and interest are causing the cash to grow, the death benefit is increasing as well. The highest amount of death benefit is $530,402 in year fifteen, which is also the year she paid the highest price for insurance: $739.

Index Life Contract Illustration

Year	Age	Sp Age	Ann Prem	Acct Val	Surrender Val	Death Benefit	COI
11	56	11	$12,000	$169,146	$169,146	$422,123	$456
12	57	12	$12,000	$193,460	$193,460	$446,437	$513
13	58	13	$12,000	$219,528	$219,528	$472,505	$579
14	59	14	$12,000	$247,472	$247,742	$500,449	$655
15	60	15	$12,000	$277,425	$277,425	$530,402	$739
16	61	16		$297,690	$297,690	$386,997	$431
17	62	17		$319,422	$319,422	$408,861	$481
18	63	18		$342,726	$342,726	$431,835	$538

But then notice year sixteen. That's when her death benefit reduces to $386,997. This can be done because no more premiums will be added to the policy. Once the Guideline Single Premium is met, the policy owner can choose to either drop the death benefit or continue to deposit premiums. Since this policy owner wanted to maximize cash value, she dropped the death benefit which tightened the corridor (as you can see in the line graph on page 109). As her cash value continued to increase through interest earnings, the death benefit increased accordingly. Her earnings are optimized.

You can also see that the policy was the most expensive the first five years when the cost of the insurance was at its highest. She is depositing premiums, but her account value is less than the premiums paid in. She hasn't lost money in the market; the cost of the insurance is high, so it is taking more of her premium to cover those costs. Her break-even point is in year five. She has put in $60,000 in premium and her account value is $60,000. From that point forward, the cash value of the policy is growing larger than the premiums she has paid in.

When she reaches maximum efficiency in year seventeen, the actual rate of return is 5.44 percent. From that point forward, the value of the account increases each year. The 5.44 percent, it is interesting to note, is the overall return for the first sixteen years of the policy. By the twenty-first year or at age sixty-six, the contract averaged over 6 percent from inception. This is an important number to know. I ran this life insurance illustration at 7.50 percent. If the overall return in year twenty-one is showing a 6 percent actual rate of return, this means the average cost of this contract each year from inception is only 1.50 percent. This 1.50 percent cost includes the cost of the death benefit each year and the management of the funds. This is a lot less than what it would cost for a term life insurance policy plus paying any equity-based institution to manage an account this size.

When the policy holder minimized the death benefit and maximized the premium, she minimized the internal cost of the contract so that she could accumulate tax-favored cash for future use. Her retirement years will be much less financially stressful because she chose this option, but in the case of premature death, her loved ones will have the death benefit to help them through the loss.

Comparing Costs

Okay, now that you understand costs and the corridor, you can now better understand the comparison between an IUL policy and an equity account in terms of costs.

Here is the same woman's policy we've been discussing. It shows the costs as I noted above on the top chart. The next chart shows the costs to an equity account that is funded with the same $12,000 a year for fifteen years. The third chart shows the comparison between the two. This hypothetical equity account charges a conservative 1 percent management fee (they are usually more than 1 percent), and a 28 percent federal income tax.

Index Universal Life Policy Charges and Expense Detail

Year	Age	Plan Prem	Prem Chg	Pol Fee	Unit Chg	COI	Total
1	46	$12,000	$600	$90	$1,226	$450	$2,366
2	47	$12,000	$600	$90	$1,226	$492	$2,409
3	48	$12,000	$600	$90	$1,226	$527	$2,444
4	49	$12,000	$600	$90	$1,226	$555	$2,471
5	50	$12,000	$600	$90	$1,226	$590	$2,506
6	51	$12,000	$600	$90	$1,226	$563	$2,479
7	52	$12,000	$600	$90	$1,226	$537	$2,453
8	53	$12,000	$600	$90	$1,226	$505	$2,421
9	54	$12,000	$600	$90	$1,226	$463	$2,379
10	55	$12,000	$600	$90	$1,226	$408	$2,325
TOT		$120,000	$6,000	$900	$12,260	$5,090	$24,253
11	56	$12,000	$600	$90	$0	$456	$1,146
12	57	$12,000	$600	$90	$0	$513	$1,203
13	58	$12,000	$600	$90	$0	$579	$1,269
14	59	$12,000	$600	$90	$0	$655	$1,345
15	60	$12,000	$600	$90	$0	$739	$1,429
16	61	$0	$0	$90	$0	$431	$521
17	62	$0	$0	$90	$0	$481	$571
18	63	$0	$0	$90	$0	$538	$628
19	64	$0	$0	$90	$0	$597	$687
20	65	$0	$0	$90	$0	$656	$746
TOT		$180,000	$9,000	$1,800	$12,260	$10,735	$33,798

Equity Account Charges and Expense Detail*

Deposits	S&P Ret	Gains/Loss	Tax	Mgmt Fee	Term Cost	Total
$12,000	31.57%	$3,751	-$174	-$120	$0	-$294
$12,000	18.56%	$5,103	-$300	-$326	$0	-$626
$12,000	5.10%	$2,243	-$373	-$462	$0	-$835
$12,000	16.61%	$9,531	-$668	-$669	$0	-$1,337
$12,000	31.69%	$24,583	-$952	-$1,022	$0	-$1,974
$12,000	-3.10%	-$3,478	-$1,076	-$1,087	$0	-$2,163
$12,000	30.47%	$36,119	-$1,366	-$1,547	$0	-$2,913
$12,000	7.62%	$12,478	-$1,433	-$1,762	$0	-$3,195
$12,000	10.08%	$18,651	-$1,547	-$2,037	$0	-$3,584
$12,000	1.32%	$2,800	-$1,681	-$2,149	$0	-$3,830
TOT			-$9,570	-$11,181	$0	-$20,751
$12,000	37.58%	$83,828	-$2,137	-$3,069	$0	-$5,206
$12,000	22.96%	$72,022	-$2,342	-$3,857	$0	-$6,199
$12,000	33.36%	$130,608	-$2,542	-$5,221	$0	-$7,763
$12,000	28.58%	$150,432	-$2,750	-$6,768	$0	-$9,518
$12,000	21.04%	$142,918	-$2,875	-$8,222	$0	-$11,097
	-9.10%	-$73,809	-$2,340	-$7,373	$0	-$9,713
	-11.89%	-$86,508	-$2,322	-$6,411	$0	-$8,733
	-22.10%	-$139,744	-$2,231	-$4,926	$0	-$7,157
	28.69%	$139,269	-$3,099	-$6,247	$0	-$9,346
	10.88%	$66,950	-$3,220	-$6,823	$0	-$10,043
			-$35,428	-$70,098	$0	-$105,526

*These returns include dividends, and dividends are taxed.

Comparison

Policy Cost	Invest Cost	Year	Difference
$2,366	$294	1	
$4,775	$920	2	
$7,219	$1,755	3	
$9,690	$3,092	4	
$12,196	$5,066	5	
$14,675	$7,229	6	
$17,128	$10,142	7	
$19,549	$13,337	8	
$21,928	$16,921	9	
$24,253	$20,751	10	
$25,399	$25,957	11	$558
$26,602	$32,156	12	$5,554
$27,871	$39,919	13	$12,048
$29,216	$49,437	14	$20,221
$30,645	$60,534	15	$29,889
$31,166	$70,247	16	$39,081
$31,737	$78,980	17	$47,243
$32,365	$86,137	18	$53,772
$33,052	$95,483	19	$62,431
$33,798	$105,526	20	$71,728

When you compare the cost of the S&P Equity Index scenario to an Index UL contract, you can see out of the gate the IUL policy is more expensive per year. This is one of the reasons why most people will not use these contracts for accumulation. They are not willing to wait long enough to take advantage of the cost cross over—when the account is making more than it is costing the policy owner. This happens in year five, as I have already pointed out above. But look at year eleven. The policy owner is paying more for her equity account than she is for insurance.

Now look at the first ten years. The total cost for the insurance policy is $24,253; the total cost for the equity account is $20,751. The management fee is deducted from your equity account annually, just as the four costs are deducted annually in an insurance contract. But you have to pay the taxes directly to the government. That potentially is a hefty out-of-pocket expense. Furthermore, the $20,751 is assuming that the owner of the equity account has not purchased any term insurance. If they did, they would have a consistent cost in that category, every year. Say that's $900 annually; that increases the amount on the equity side to $29,751 for the first ten years.

So if you had to pay fees, taxes, and term insurance on the equity side, you would actually save about $5,000 in costs on the IUL side.

However, look at the cost difference between the IUL and the equity account in year twenty (when this woman would now be sixty five and ready to start taking out distributions.) She has paid a total of $33,798 for the cost of insurance for those twenty years. If she would have had her money in an equity account, her total cost of ownership would be in the range of $105,526 if she didn't pay for a term life policy. If she did, you could add another $18,000 to that $105,00, for a total of $123,526.

That is a startling difference: a potential $89,728 of additional cumulated cost in an equity account. That's money that could be in an IUL contract earning compounding interest with a cap and floor, enjoying the reset and lock-in features. It is money that you could have available to you when you need it most in your later years. The IUL gains are never taxed, the account value is not subject to market risk, *and*, since an integral part of the IUL contract is the death benefit, you would leave a legacy to your heirs, tax-free. If you were in the equity market, you may have a term life insurance policy. But most people let that lapse around their retirement years because term is too expensive to renew. So they miss out on leaving a tax-free legacy.

So yes, an IUL policy is more expensive out of the gate, but I and many others gladly pay the upfront costs to enjoy all the benefits on the back end. To give you a snapshot of a later year's activity: this woman paid $481 for insurance in year seventeen when she earned $21,000, in interest that year tax-free. Her account value in year seventeen is $319,000. If she had her money in an equity account, she would have to pay annual taxes on the $21,000, and she would have to pay her fund manager's fee on the entire $319,000. If her fund manager was charging a 1 percent fee, she would owe him or her around $3,000. If she found a very generous manager who only charged her a half point (.5 percent), that's still $1,500. So with a conservative money-manager fee of half a point, and giving the IRS the benefit of the doubt of only charging 20 percent for income taxes on the gains, the total cost that year on an equity account would be around $5,795 not $481 as it is in the IUL.

It's like the old oil filter TV commercial years ago. The salesman comes out on the TV screen with a filter in his hand. There's a car behind him with blue smoke rolling out of the hood. The salesman looks square in the camera and says, "You can pay me now, or pay dearly later." You can either pay the cost of permanent life insurance up front or pay more as the years roll by in an equity account.

With an IUL contract, you must pay for the backend performance up front. But you get to watch it transform into something really great if you're patient.

I said in chapter 5 that there are a number of moving parts in a life insurance contract. I have spent the last four chapters explaining to you how your money grows, how it goes in and out of a life insurance contract, and how much you pay for the peace of mind you get with an IUL policy.

Most people will not take the time to understand how these parts all work together. This is one of the reasons why our government hasn't put any more restrictions on these contracts than they already have. Since most Americans do not take the time to learn the benefits of these contracts and use them, there isn't a sense of urgency by the regulatory authorities to excessively monitor these products.

However, more and more people are starting to study and realize the benefits and uses for the IUL. I believe there will come a time when these contracts will be so widely utilized for retirement planning and other financial purposes, they will get the attention of law makers, and some compromises to the tax codes and federal laws will be made. But for now we have an opportunity to use the current laws to capitalize on a great product. I have shown you the basics; you're now armed with workable knowledge. It is up to you to put it into practice.

To find a local Family Financial Miracle Representative, please visit www.FFMRegistry.com.

9 The Most Powerful Institutions on Earth

If you fall, you hope that you have a cushion, preferably one that's large enough that you won't feel any pain. When the risk of falling is high, you hope you have a bigger cushion under you to break the fall. The idea of insurance was started as a way to spread the amount of risk—for money, fires, accidents or what have you—to a group of individuals instead of just one person. The idea is that it lessens the pain if there is loss or harm.

I have spent the entire book talking about how your money inside an Index Universal Life contract is protected because of the cap and floor features with lock-in and reset. However, what ensures that protection is the way in which insurance companies do business. They are required by law to protect your money in ways no other institutions can come close to matching.

Insurance companies have been around since the early sixteen hundreds when groups of merchants and ship owners would gather in a coffee shop in London owned by Edward Lloyd. They came specifically seeking insurance for the cargo they were ferrying back and forth from the New World. These ships were at risk of getting lost or destroyed. Merchants would mitigate the risk by dividing their cargo amongst several boats. They were protected from complete loss that way, but they added another layer of protection with insurance. Before a ship would set sail, the merchants and ship owners would go to Lloyds to meet with the investors, those who took on the risk of the voyage for a set premium. They would sign at the bottom of the manifest (hence "underwriting") indicating what share of the cargo they were taking responsibility for. There were a number of these "underwriters" for each voyage because no one person wanted to be responsible for the entire cargo. (Lloyd went on to found Lloyds of London, the premier company that handles specialty insurance.)

When the great fire of London of 1666 destroyed around fourteen thousand buildings, many found themselves without homes. In response to the tragedy—made worse by the devastation of the plague that had swept through the city a year earlier—groups of underwriters who had dealt only with marine insurance formed companies that offered fire insurance. They were helped by a man named Blaise Pascal, who had invented the first calculator, and his friend Pierre de Fermat, who together devised a way to calculate probabilities. This led to the first actuary tables which are the same mortality tables insurance companies use to calculate the cost of insurance.[28]

Life insurance companies have evolved over the years. In the middle 1800s, a man named Elizur Wright became America's first state insurance regulator in Massachusetts. His family helped fugitive slaves; he went to school with John Brown and ran an abolitionist newspaper. When he visited London, he watched old men auctioning off their policies they had paid faithfully into all their lives. They were too old to work, and so they auctioned off their death benefit to the highest bidder. It sickened Wright, who came back to America campaigning for life insurance reform. The main issue: requiring insurance companies to pay surrender values and to hold adequate reserves to do so.[29] He was also a mathematician, and he figured out how to calculate the reserves, thereby setting the very strict, ethical standards under which insurance companies operate.

Wright's reforms turned the insurance industry into some of the most powerful and safest financial institutions on earth. They are both very good at handling risk, and they have massive amounts of reserves that give them a very deep cushion, possibly the best. Think about it. When there's a massive flood or fire or hurricane, the insurance companies, not the banks, are there paying out claims and helping people rebuild their lives.

Bank Failure Rate

One of the best indicators of the insurance industry's soundness is bank failures. Since 2008, according to the Federal Deposit Insurance Corporation (FDIC), 506 banks have failed.[30] Life insurance companies, it can be argued, don't ever fail. If they get into trouble, they are considered insolvent, meaning they cannot pay their liabilities—their policy commitments. When this happens, another life insurance company will take over the assets and liabilities of the troubled company. The new company honors the policies of the former company, including the death benefit. Failed banks, too, are sold, a move facilitated by the FDIC who also insures deposits up to $250,000. However, the difference between failed banks and insurance companies is notable. Since 2008, 155 insurance companies have gone into receivership.[31] In other words, for every one insurance company faltering, roughly five banks fail.

Banks fail for a number of reasons: bad loans, bad investments on their assets, or bad management, just to name a few. Life insurance companies suffer insolvencies for one reason: under reserving.[32] Banks operate on what's called a fractional reserve system, which means that each institution is required by federal law to hold reserves equal to a certain fraction of specified types of deposits. These required reserves can be held either as vault cash (currency on hand) or as deposits at a Federal Reserve Bank. The FDIC operates on a 4 to 10 percent reserve requirement.

If a bank receives a deposit, say $1,000, the bank is required to put up to 10 percent in reserves, or $100. The remaining $900 constitutes excess reserves for the bank and is available for loans. Because the bulk of a bank's loans are made by crediting the customer-borrower's deposit account, the loan in fact becomes new deposit money.

Here's how it works. Let's say you take a $900 loan from Bank A. You pay a merchant $900 for a computer. The merchant deposits the $900 in Bank B. That bank then puts 10 percent in reserves and can loan out the $810. In the meantime, you are making payments on your loan. Every time you send a payment, say $100, the bank keeps $10 and loans out $90.

This process of money creation continues until total deposits amount to a multiple of the reserves supplied to the banking system by the Federal Reserve, where the multiple is determined by the required reserve ratio.

The illustration below shows how an initial deposit of a $1,000 Social Security check at a commercial bank can generate an additional $9,000 of deposits in the banking system under the assumption of a reserve ratio of 10 percent. That $9,000 was created not from an account earning interest; the money is just being loaned to person A and deposited by person B over and over again at the 10/90 ratio of reserves-to-new-loan monies.

Stage	Amount Deposited	Required Services	Excess Reserves	Loan and Investment Money Created
Initial Deposit	$1,000.00	$100.00	$900.00	$900.00
Stage 1	$900.00	$90.00	$810.00	$810.00
Stage 2	$810.00	$81.00	$729.00	$729.00
Stage 3	$729.00	$72.90	$656.10	$656.10
Stage 4	$656.10	$65.61	$590.49	$590.49
Stage 5	$590.49	$59.05	$531.44	$531.44
Stage 6	$531.44	$53.14	$478.30	$478.30
Stage 7	$478.30	$47.83	$430.47	$430.47
Stage 8	$430.47	$43.05	$387.42	$387.42
Stage 9	$387.42	$38.74	$348.68	$348.68
All Others	$3,486.78	$348.68	$3,138.10	$3,138.10
Total	$10,000.00	$1,000.00	$9,000.00	$9,000.00

P-38   Public Affairs Federal Reserve Bank of Richmond 5/93
P.O. Box 27622, Richmond, Virginia 32361

What happens to the money in reserves? Part of it is invested. If it were all invested in highly volatile, speculative vehicles that would make banks very unsafe. Rather, banks put part of their reserve in very safe vehicles. Bank-owned life insurance (BOLI) is one of the fastest growing assets for a bank's "tier one" money. Tier one is the foundation, the money that needs to be put in the safest places possible. This should make anyone pause. Why would banks tell us to put money in a bank vehicle when they are storing their own reserves in permanent life insurance? Because permanent life insurance carriers do not operate on a fractional reserve system.

Permanent life insurance companies are required, by federal and state law, to have dollar-for-dollar reserves.

The General Fund

All insurance companies work out of a general fund or general account, and the money we pay to our insurance company as premiums goes into its general account. That account is highly regulated which means the rules under which it is managed are very strict. Furthermore, insurance companies are held highly accountable for that money. Why? Because the insurance company is a fiduciary; they are entrusted with your money and must handle it for your future benefit not for their own profit. Because of this, an insurance company must submit a hefty annual report to all the states it operates in, and the general account is also audited every year. This is very close scrutiny.

The person responsible for managing the general fund is the Chief Investment Officer of the insurance company. The Chief Investment Officer is a highly skilled person because these general accounts tend to be enormous. For example one of the carriers I use has a general account of $120 billion. Its total amount of liabilities is $113.5 billion; that is the amount of money they would have to pay out if everyone made a claim on their policies at one time. They have $7.7 billion in equity accounts.

An insurance company is responsible for investing the funds in their general account, and a percentage of the investments are put in safe vehicles. These general account investments earn an average of 5 to 8 percent, and they have done this consistently for upwards of two hundred years. If an insurance company's general account is $120 billion, 5 percent is $6 billon. From this 5 to 8 percent interest the general account earns comes the interest credited to your cash value in your life insurance policy.

Let's say the general account earns 6 percent interest. Keep in mind this is $120 billion earning 6 percent. The insurance company allocates about 1 percent of their earnings (in this example around $1 billion) to manage operations and administrative costs. These dollars keep the company running proficiently. Another one percent is allocated toward company profits. The remaining 4 percent is what is allocated to support and pay the returns on the company's fixed accounts for their permanent life insurance portfolio. If the general account is crediting 7 percent in one year, the fixed account will be 5 percent. If the general account is crediting 5 percent, the fixed account will go down to 3 percent. The percentage of interest being earned by the insurance company's well-balanced general account dictates what interest rate is available for the company's life insurance fixed portfolio.

The Index Option

Let's assume a 6 percent gross in the general account, netting 4 percent after administrative costs and profits have been paid. This 4 percent can be used by the insurance company to do different things in an Index Universal Life policy. As I just explained, the insurance company can guarantee you a 4 percent fixed rate of return on your cash value if you choose the fixed allocation to place your money in that year. Let's say I have $100,000 in my IUL cash value. I choose the 4 percent fixed allocation. This is the 4 percent left over after the administrative costs and the profits are taken from the earning on the general account. At the end of the year I would receive a guaranteed 4 percent credit. My cash value is now $104,000.

However, the insurance company can also take that 4 percent to an options trader to purchase an equity index option if the index allocation is what you chose for your money.

This is how the insurance company sets the indexed allocation cap every year. That 4 percent, or $4,000 on your $100,000, allows the insurance company to buy an equity index option with a cap (options are financial strategies used in market trading). They aren't putting the money *in* the equity index, they're just purchasing the ability to participate in the index gain. The cap is predicated on the price of the option for any particular year. The insurance company is not setting the cap, the options trader is. One year, the options trader is selling the cap at 12 percent for the $4,000; the next year, 14 percent. But maybe the next year the options trader is selling the cap for only 11 percent. The insurance company will always use whatever the fixed account is crediting to buy whatever cap the options trader is selling.

The only thing you are putting at risk is the 4 percent you would have earned if you placed the $100,000 in the fixed allocation (and keep in mind you are never risking any of your principal—in this case $100,000).

When the insurance company takes the 4 percent it was going to pay me and buys a cap of 12 percent and a floor of 0 percent for an S&P Index allocation, then your cap is set. What happens next is what I explained in chapter 5. If the S&P Index is down at all for the next twelve months, I would not have any interest credited to my cash value, but I wouldn't lose any money either. If the market goes up, two things can happen. If the market is up less than the annual cap, for example the index increases by 5 percent, I would get 5 percent credited to my cash. If the index rises 20 percent, because the annual cap is set at 12 percent, I receive 12 percent interest, in this case $12,000.

There is a misconception that the option trader or the insurance company gets the difference between the 12 percent cap and the amount the index increases above the 12 percent cap. This just isn't true. The 4 percent that could have been credited to my cash from the fixed allocation was exhausted purchasing the largest cap available that year, 12 percent, from the options trader. If the 4 percent interest from my cash value can purchase a higher cap, the insurance company has the incentive to purchase the highest cap available for that year but not for them, for their policy holders. They are going to spend the entire 4 percent no matter what, so whatever they can purchase as a cap for that year with the 4 percent, that is what they will do. Any increase in an index above the policy equity index cap in any given year doesn't benefit anyone.

The State Guarantee Fund

The insurance industry is quite a phenomenon actually. No matter what is happening in the world—wars, recessions or depressions, sweeping epidemics, inflation or deflation—insurance companies have protected people to a degree unmatched by any other type of financial institution in the world. During the Great Depression of 1929 to 1938, when around nine thousand banks either failed or had their operations suspended, 99 percent of all life insurance policies continued unaffected. Those who had money in the 1 percent of affected companies were still safe because even back then, provisions were in place to handle the problem through acquisitions and mergers.

It's also interesting to note that no matter the size of an insurance company, it is a tower of financial stability. In 1949, Leroy Lincoln, President of Metropolitan Life of New York (at the time the largest life insurance carrier in the world) said, "You're as safe and as well protected…if you buy from a small insurance company as from the largest." [33]

The first layer of safety is the way in which money from the general fund is invested. The second layer comes from the reserves every insurance company is required to maintain. Above I said there is a dollar-for-dollar system in place. This constitutes something called the "Legal Reserve System" that is put in place by the State Guarantee Fund.

Each state in the U.S. has its own state insurance department that acts on its own laws and regulations. It supervises all aspects of an insurance company's operation within that state including approving policy forms and even in some cases sales material before it can be offered to the public. It reviews complaints as well as all mergers of companies doing business within its boundaries. The state in which an insurance company does business charges a tax to the insurance company to do business in that state. This is what the "load" or premium fee covers in your insurance costs as you are putting in, or "loading" your premium.

All states require insurance companies doing business there to have the dollar-for-dollar reserves to cover their liabilities. The liability is the cash value in a life insurance policy. So if your cash value is $100,000, the insurance company has to keep that same amount in reserve. Banks, I have pointed out, are only required to have ten cents on the dollar for liabilities. On top of that, the highest rated insurance companies often carry surpluses in their reserves.

I noted above that under-reserving is the only way insurance companies fail. How can that be if they have to keep such massive reserves in their general account? It really comes down to poor money management. Even with stringent rules and regulations, some insurance companies find ways around them, but when they do, they suffer.

If you are looking to buy a life insurance policy, it is vital that you find out what their ratings are. All insurance companies have at least three different ratings they publish. One of the carriers we use lists Standard & Poor's (the same ones that give us the S&P index), A.M Best, and Moody's. When you consider an insurance company, you want to see "A" to "A+" ratings. If there is an A-, it should be offset with A+ ratings elsewhere. If you see "B" ratings, it means that they are not handling their reserves conservatively enough. They are taking too much investment risk and thus their general fund is at risk.

Insuring Conservatively

Insurance companies have a stellar reputation on purpose. If they weren't ultra conservative with the money you send them in premiums, you wouldn't trust them. There would be no insurance business if that were the case.

This is why they are also conservative when it comes to who they actually insure. There are three entities involved in an insurance contract: the owner of the policy, the insured, and the beneficiary.

Remember the builder and his wife who lost all their retirement money in their son's failed condo development project? When he came to me three years after he purchased the original policy distraught because his son's business venture was failing, he told me that he wasn't able to fund the original policy. He asked me what he could do because he wanted to protect the remaining money he had left. Unfortunately, because he had developed congestive heart failure and adult-onset diabetes, he was no longer eligible for a policy. He wasn't healthy enough.

Life insurance is about insuring your life against premature death. If you have a higher probability of dying, the company will not insure you. There are ways around this issue: if you're the owner, you can purchase an insurance policy on your spouse, your children, or your grandchildren, and you can name whomever you want as a beneficiary. The owner of the policy has access to the cash value of the contract and has the right to make changes to the contract. These are details you will need to work out with a licensed agent.

There are the naysayers out there who do not understand the financial strength of insurance companies. They have not looked at the rigorous federal and state requirements by which these institutions are regulated. Insurance companies rarely make poor decisions about how they manage their general funds. You, however, never need to worry about being adversely affected if this does occur because of the laws under which all insurance companies must abide. Index Universal Life insurance is my family's financial miracle precisely because my money is so protected in my insurance company's many layers of reserves and guarantees.

To find a local Family Financial Miracle Representative, please visit www.FFMRegistry.com.

10 Mastering the Possibilities

In the end, the possibilities an Index Universal Life policy offers is really about cash flow. When I said at the beginning that money is like air—you need it to live in our world just as much as you need air—it's money that is available to use when you need it most. If your washer breaks down, you go to the appliance store and buy one if you have cash flow. If your children want to go to summer camp, or your grandchildren want to come visit you, and you have ready cash, you can make that happen for them.

The less your cash flow is impeded, the more flexibility you have for maintaining your lifestyle. When you retire, being able to take distributions without major tax penalties and having access to your cash through IUL policy loans can mean the difference between maintaining a comfortable living or suffering through your retirement on a dreaded fixed income.

An Index Universal Life contract, when it is built to optimize cash accumulation, offers possibilities that I have yet to see rivaled by any other savings vehicle. You have seen many of them already: the heiress who learned that with an IUL policy she could leave a legacy without suffocating on a massive tax bill every year; the doctor who learned that if he collateralized his cash with an IUL policy loan, his money could be doing two things at once including earning interest in an investment while still earning interest inside the policy. That and he wouldn't zero out his savings in his retirement.

What I have learned over the past twelve years of helping people is that maintaining financial balance is essential to creating your own family financial miracle. Here's what I mean.

Mortgages: How many of you are thinking about going to a fifteen-year mortgage? You want to pay your mortgage off sooner under the assumption you are paying less interest. But when you go into a fifteen-year mortgage, what happens to your payments? They increase by at least a third, which decreases your cash flow—cash flow that could be going in a safe and accessible place earning tax free interest and providing a death benefit to pay off the mortgage if you die. How often have you heard someone being "house rich, but cash poor"? They have a fabulous asset in their home, but they are unable to take out an equity line of credit for whatever reason: poor credit score or not enough income for example.

Perhaps they don't want to take a line of credit because they learned in their youth that's dangerous. I know an elderly woman who is sitting on a million dollar property she and her husband bought for $11,000 in 1961. Thirty years later their sleepy little town became one of America's best places to raise a family. That sounds like an incredible investment, until you calculate the rate of return. If you compound $11,000 at 8.71 percent for fifty four years, it becomes a million bucks. However, this widow is on a fixed income. The bank will not allow her to take any major lines of credit, and she doesn't want to because she doesn't want to be saddled with payments. She refuses to use a reverse mortgage because she doesn't like them. She is most definitely house rich but cash poor. What are her options?

She's still within the age limit of taking out an IUL policy. She's healthy, so if she is ready to give up her home, she could sell it, put half the cash into an IUL and the other half into a bank account that she could live off comfortably for the remaining years of her life. She would have a policy from which she could withdraw funds if needed, and her five children would have at least the same amount of legacy as they would if she kept the home and they sold it when she passed away.

Real estate can be a very lucrative investment. Your home is an asset that can work very well for you if you know how to effectively manage the cash flow from it. Let's go back to the fifteen-year mortgage. I advise my clients to hold off and keep the thirty year mortgage. Then take the difference in the payments on the fifteen year mortgage and fund an IUL policy. The premiums and interest earned can normally pay off that thirty year mortgage in thirteen years if that is what the client wants to do with the accumulated dollars. However, when it comes time to write the check from the policy to pay off the remaining mortgage, most of my clients who have taken the IUL route don't do it. They keep on paying the thirty-year mortgage payment and enjoy the freedom of having access to the accumulated cash. The IUL you fund from the money redirected from the fifteen year mortgage could generate enough cash flow to fund a rental property or a vacation home.

Cars or other capital purchases can work the same way. Jim O, the Virginia Hall-of-Fame Shagger, totally shifted his viewpoint when I showed him how you can make money by not buying cars or such outright. He was the man who moved his money in other permanent life insurance products into IUL policies. He's been making a steady 6 to 7 percent rate or return since he purchased them in 2002.

He wanted to buy a new truck. I showed him how he could collateralize his cash in the IUL policy to purchase the truck for 2 percent from the car dealer and still make the 6 to 7 percent on his money. If he paid for the car outright, he would be losing money because he wouldn't still have the collateralized cash earning interest in the policy. It was quite the paradigm shift for him, but once he got it, he embraced the idea wholeheartedly. This is what he told me: "I like many others grew up with the theory that you own all you have. I lived through the Great Depression and saw what it was like to lose everything. So the prevailing idea was, when you purchase something, pay it off in as short a time as possible if you can't buy it outright. I still run into people who refuse to think any differently than 'I want to own what I got.' When I finally got it straight that I could still make money in my IUL policy while I purchased what I needed, I was tickled. Now I'm not interested in owning it; I'm interested in using it." Jim has never paid cash outright for a car or other major purchases since.

Index Universal Life contracts offer a wealth of applications. Take the couple who didn't know what to do with an errant brother. My client was fifty-five, his wife was about the same age at the time this all happened. He had taken out a policy with a $250,000 Guideline Single Premium and a death benefit of $850,000 four years prior. He wanted to see how much money he had in the policy. I pulled up his statement. It had $185,000 in premiums. He needed to put two more premiums in and then it would be done. He had also earned interest on his premiums, and the cash value in his policy was $210,000. He had the $66,000 he needed to fund the rest of the policy, but he was waiting until he saw how the contract was performing before he made the next premium payment. When I showed him and his wife that he had lost about $8,000 on his $60,000 by waiting because the market was doing well and he would have earned his cap in interest, his wife looked at him and said, "why did you do that?!"

We had a good chuckle, and then the husband told me this story: He's got a dead-beat brother who lives in his dad's house. His dad is ninety-two, and the responsible brother, my client, just put his dad in a nursing home. He told me that his brother has always lived off their dad. He's never held a job so he's never paid into Social Security. "What am I going to do?" he asked me. "I feel obligated to take care of him because he's my brother. I'm thinking about renting out my dad's house and using the proceeds from the rent to give my brother $1,000 a month to live on."

I asked him, "Do you really want to be a landlord?" My client didn't like that idea, so I suggested this: "Sell your dad's house." (It was worth about $280,000.) "Hold back enough for your brother to live on for the next three years at $1,000 a month, or $36,000. Buy an IUL policy on the brother by placing the rest of the funds from the sale of the house in an IUL contract—in other words, MEC that contract. You will own the policy on your brother and make your kids the beneficiaries of the death benefit. In three years, you can start taking policy loans from the IUL for him to live on. You've allowed the policy three full years to grow untouched, so there should be enough cash in the policy to create enough annual interest using the fixed allocation to make the $12,000 annual payments to your brother to live on. This most likely will not deplete the value of policy in your brother's lifetime. You don't have to deal with being a landlord, and when your brother dies, you get the money back from the death benefit, tax-free, to give to your children. By handling it this way, you don't have to be a landlord. You take care of your brother, and your dad provides a legacy for his grandchildren and avoids any gift tax."

My client really liked that idea, and it is one of thousands of stories that show how flexible yet useful an IUL policy can be and how it allows you to retain control of your money.

From time to time, I'll have someone ask, "Do you sell life insurance?" I tell them no. I never sell life insurance. What I do is proudly buy it for my clients. I find them the right company that has the right product that does the right thing for the right application. I teach my clients how to control their money by paying attention to the market so they know how to choose the best allocation for their money for the year. I have trained them so well that when the market falls, they call me. They're not upset; they're excited.

They know that their money isn't losing anything because of the fixed floor. They know their gains are locked in from the previous year and that the index values will be reset at the new lower value once their anniversary comes up. That annual reset will allow them to potentially make the full capped returns the next year on their money. If the cap is 12 percent, and they didn't make any money in one year, they know they could possibly make 12 percent the next year. They love that—and then they ask me again, "Wow, how did you know my account would average 6 percent?"

Over the past fifteen years, I have been helping people manage their savings using Index Universal Life insurance policies. I have had clients pass away and their heirs receive the death benefits. One of my clients that this happened to is named Phyllis. When she and her husband wanted to meet me, I decided to make a house call. They lived in a beautiful older home, built in the early 1950s, and it was situated on Chesapeake Bay. It had a gorgeous view on a large waterfront lot. When you live near large bodies of water, your house tends to take a beating. Phyllis will tell you the house needed work. But that wasn't the problem. Taxes were. Her property tax had skyrocketed. When they bought the house in the mid-1960s, they only paid $50,000 and their property tax was around $100. Forty years later, she was paying close to $9,000. Her husband was in real estate, and she was ready to move. She told him to go find a one-story condo.

This happened in late 2006. I helped them understand by selling their home and putting a large part of the cash from the sale into an IUL policy, it would provide them more liquidity, use and control over their money. I suggested they put a quarter of the money made from the sale of the house in a policy on her, and three quarters of the money in a policy on him.

They also had taxable investments all over the place and were highly exposed to market risk. I took most of that money and put it into a fixed annuity and annuitized it so it would pay out a monthly income for the rest of their lives.

They had a buyer by January 2007, but it took him three months to close. They moved into their condo in July of 2007. In January of 2008, I went to visit Phyllis and her husband, Jim. He had been out playing tennis but came home not feeling well. Within a few days, he had died unexpectedly. Phyllis called me with the bad news. I was devastated as I put through the death claim. It was a million dollars.

When I delivered her claim, she needed to know what she should do with it. When they bought the condo, I advised them to finance it, but if they needed to pay it off, they could do so with a policy loan. Since I knew her home was secure, I advised her to take half of the money, $500,000, and buy a modified endowment contract. She didn't need the money; it was primarily there as a legacy for her daughter, so she wouldn't be taking loans on the policy. I also told her she should go buy a car. She was set financially for the rest of her life. She was always very frugal with her money and had over a million dollars sitting in bank accounts and life insurance policies. She went out and bought her fun car—a white convertible V.W.—and has loved it ever since.

She told me once, "If it weren't for you, Merle, I would be in such a financial mess. The house had problems and would have been expensive to fix. It is such a blessing that this came along. I'm financially comfortable. I don't have to worry, and I know what that's like. I've been every which direction with money. I'm so appreciative of what you've done. People need to realize this—it's not about the money, it's about the help."

I consider my clients my friends. With Index Universal Life, I know that I can help give them a bright financial future, one with little worry and, I hope, many blessings.

You will read things on the internet and hear from other financial advisors that Index Universal Life policies aren't what they promise. Remember, not all policies are created equal. They have different provisions; some outperform others based on how the contract is written. You need to do your own homework and make up your own mind about what you read. Ask yourself, is it opinion or fact?

As I have said throughout, my family financial miracle can be yours. I encourage you to take the next steps and find out how you can enjoy the three family financial principles: growth, protection, and income through liquidity, use, and control.

I hope you enjoyed reading this book as much as I enjoyed writing it because I truly believe that Index Universal Life products can help many, many people. Even if you never use what you learned personally, please make sure what you read isn't wasted. This information really can change someone's life.

Endnotes

Notes Chapter 2

1   Alicia H. Munnell and Matthew S. Rutledge. "The Effects of the Great Recession on the Retirement Security of Older Workers." Boston: National Poverty Center, March 2015 (5).

    For all references to the S&P®, S&P 500®, the Dow®, the Down Jones®: This book is not sponsored, endorsed, sold or promoted by S&P Dow Jones Indices LLC (SPDJI), Dow Jones®, S&P 500®, their respective affiliates, and none of such parties make any representation regarding the advisability of investing in such product(s) nor do they have any liability for any errors, omissions, or interruptions of the S&P 500 or the Dow Jones Industrial Average. "S&P 500" and the "Dow Jones Industrial Average" are products of S&P Dow Jones Indices LLC ("SPDJI"). Standard & Poor's®, S&P® and S&P 500® are registered trademarks of Standard & Poor's Financial Services LLC ("S&P"); DJIA®, The Dow®, Dow Jones® and Dow Jones Industrial Average are trademarks of Dow Jones Trademark Holdings LLC ("Dow Jones"); and these trademarks have been licensed for use by SPDJI.

2   John Carney. "America Lost $10.2 Trillion In 2008." Feb. 3, 2009, accessed March 26, 2015. http://www.businessinsider.com/2009/2/america-lost-102-trillion-of-wealth-in-2008.

3   Older Poor Americans and Their Search for Work. *Here and Now with Robin Young and Jeremy Hobson. July 30, 2014, accessed March 26, 2015.* http://hereandnow.wbur.org/2014/07/30/older-americans-workamping.

    Jessica Bruder. "The End of Retirement. When You Can't Afford to Stop Working." June 2, 2015, accessed March 26, 2015. http://harpers.org/archive/2014/08/the-end-of-retirement/

4   Mamta Badkar. "BlackRock's Got A Great Chart Of The Emotional Investing Roller Coaster". Accessed March 26, 2015. http://www.businessinsider.com/financial-advisor-insights-may-31-2013-5#ixzz3Vcb8kdxZ

5   Andrew Adam Newman. "Selling Gum with Health Claims." *The New York Times*. July 27, 2009, accessed December 12, 2013. http://www.nytimes.com/2009/07/28/business/media/28adco.html?

6   Council of Economic Advisers. Posted by Jason Furman and Betsey Stevenson. February 23, 2015, accessed March 11, 2015. https://www.whitehouse.gov/blog/2015/02/23/effects-conflicted-investment-advice-retirement-savings

Notes Chapter 3

7   Jeffery Levine. "President Obama's 2016 budget targets retirement accounts." Accessed April 2, 2015. http://www.marketwatch.com/story/president-obamas-2016-budget-targets-retirement-accounts-2015-02-05.

8   Robert Steyer. "ICI: U.S. retirement assets hit record $20.8 trillion." Pensions and Investments. June 26, 2013, accessed April 2, 2015. http://www.pionline.com/article/20130626/ONLINE/130629908/ici-us-retirement-assets-hit-record-208-trillion. March 28, 2015.

9   Henry Blodget "The Truth About Taxes: Here's How High Today's Rates Really Are." July 12, 2011, accessed April 2, 2015. http://www.businessinsider.com/history-of-tax-rates. March 28, 2015.

10   David McKnight. *The Power of Zero: How to Get to the 0% Tax Bracket and Transform Your Retirement. Boston: Alcanthus Publishing, 2013 (1—3).*

11   The idea of 1 trillion seconds comes from Patrick Kelly, *The Retirement Miracle. 2011. Page 15.*

12   Bill Bischoff. "Capital gains: At what rate will your long-term sales be taxed." February 23, 2105, accessed April 3, 2015. http://www.marketwatch.com/story/capital-gains-at-what-rate-will-your-long-term-sales-be-taxed-2015-02-18.

13   Joseph Henchman. "How Many Words are in the Tax Code." April 15, 2014, accessed March 29, 2015. http://taxfoundation.org/blog/how-many-words-are-tax-code.

14   There are a large number of articles on the web that talk about state and local pensions being underfunded or bankrupt: http://www.cbo.gov/sites/default/files/05-04-pensions.pdf. http://assets.aarp.org/www.aarp.org_/articles/work/pension-funding-gap.pdf http://www.njspotlight.com/stories/14/12/03/moody-s-new-jersey-s-pension-funds-could-run-dry-in-just-10-years/.

15   Charles D. Ellis et al. *Falling Short: The Coming Retirement Crisis and What to Do About it. New York: Oxford UP, 2014 (21-24).*

16   *The Power of Zero, 17*

17   "History of Ratios." SocialSecurity.gov.http://www.ssa.gov/history/ratios. html

18   *The Power of Zero, 5 – 6.*

19   Stan Hinden. "Are My Social Security Benefits Taxable?" Feb. 10, 2014, accessed March 29, 2015. http://www.aarp.org/work/social-security/info-2014/social-security-benefit-taxes.html. March 29, 2015.

Notes Chapter 4

20   Tim Lusher. "The truth about recovering from a brain injury. June 22, 2010, accessed April 3, 2015. http://www.theguardian.com/lifeandstyle/2010/jun/22/recovering-brain-injury

21   Bryce Covert. "A Record Number of Workers Worry about Losing Their Jobs. November 26, 2013, accessed April 3, 2015. http://thinkprogress.org/economy/2013/11/26/2994771/record-worry-lose-jobs/ See also: www.washingtonpost.com/page/2010-2019/WashingtonPost/2013/09/28/National-Politics/Polling/release_266.xml

22   "My Money or Your Life." August 23, 2014, accessed April 3, 2015. http://www.economist.com/news/finance-and-economics/21613335-new-financial-instruments-may-help-make-pension-schemes-safer-my-money-or-your-life.

23   "My money or Your Life."

24   FMF. "5 Reasons to Avoid a Reverse Mortgage." December, 22, 2012, accessed April 3,2015. http://money.usnews.com/money/blogs/on-retirement/2012/12/11/5-reasons-to-avoid-a-reverse-mortgage

25   Department of Health and Human Services. "Medicaid Liens." April, 2005. Accessed April 3, 2015. http://aspe.hhs.gov/daltcp/reports/liens.htm

26   Perianne Boring. Forbes. "If you want to know the real rate of inflation, don't bother with the CPI." February 24, 2014, accessed April 3, 2015. http://www.forbes.com/sites/perianneboring/2014/02/03/if-you-want-to-know-the-real-rate-of-inflation-dont-bother-with-the-cpi/

27   Robert C. Merton. "The Crisis in Retirement Planning." Harvard Business Review. July-August 2014 (47-48).

Chapter 9 Notes

28   Andrew Beatte. "The History of Insurance." http://www.investopedia.com/articles/08/history-of-insurance.asp. Accessed April 28, 2015.

29   Actuaries Hall of Fame. Stern School of Business. New York University. http://people.stern.nyu.edu/gsimon/InsuranceHistoryPage/Wright01.pdf. Accessed April 29, 2015.

30   Failed Bank List. http://problembanklist.com/failed-bank-list/ . accessed April 29, 2014.

31   Weiss Ratings. Insurance Company Failures. http://www.weissratings.com/ratings/track-record/

32   Property/Casualty Insurance Company Insolvencies. Developed by the Financial Soundness/Risk Management Committee of the American Academy of Actuaries. September 2010. http://www.actuary.org/pdf/casualty/PC_Insurance_Company_Insolvencies_9_23_10.pdf

33   "9 Thoughts on "Are insurance company annuities insured by the government of the USA?" http://www.mortig.com/are-insurance-company-annuities-insured-by-the-government-of-the-usa/

Acknowledgements

I would like to express my deepest gratitude to the many people who I've worked with over the years to produce the content that is presented in this book, as well as the support needed to complete it.

To my mother, Patricia Reynolds, for instilling in me through your life's example the importance of honesty and hard work. They have paid off.

I wish to express gratitude to my wonderful, dedicated support team at TriQuest. Thank you Ginger McCabe, my Finance and Operations Officer, for your diligent service, brilliance, and patience.

I am especially grateful for the Eagle Team, the three men that have been with me through thick and thin: Greg Gall, Chris Lester, and Steve Buller. Thank you for sharing your ideas during the many brainstorming sessions during our careers that have contributed to this work.

I am grateful for the Triquest Base Shop leaders: John Baker and Chad Castle. Thank you for believing in me. Your dedication and hard work is vital as we have undertaken to educate the many advisors who work with us every day.

Without the wisdom and knowledge of my Chief Marketing Officer, Jeff Ziegler, this would be one of those books in the multitude of financial books lost on a shelf somewhere. Thank you for understanding how to put this important information in front of those that need it the most.

I offer special thanks to Don Blanton for his untiring commitment to educate professionals like me in the financial services industry.

Every book has a behind-the-scenes team that pushes the project through and makes it ready for the reading public. I want to thank all those who helped me see that my story could help others, who worked tirelessly through to the end helping me stay true to what I believe, who connected me to others who ensured the integrity of every word in this book. Without all your efforts and energy, this book would still just be an idea.

Most of all: to my wife, Monica Gilley. Your unconditional love and support provides the motivation and freedom I need to accomplish a level of success I would otherwise only dream about.

About the Author

 Merle Gilley is the president and founder of TriQuest USA and has been a successful life insurance agent since 2003. He has become one of the nation's leading professional trainers in the financial services industry as an Index Universal Life expert.

After serving four years in the US Air Force's Strategic Air Command (SAC) with the 93rd Bomb Wing as a B-52 crew chief, he moved back to his hometown of Virginia Beach, VA. There he met and married his wife, and together they built a successful family business. He still believes that hard work and a handshake is the best way to do business and be successful.

TriQuest USA is dedicated to helping insurance agents everywhere thoroughly understand life insurance so that they can empower people to make the best financial decisions for themselves and their families.

Gilley has spent the last decade supporting his personal client base as well as training several thousand independent financial service professionals to understand the value of working with a solid, consistent financial model and product portfolio.

For more information about Merle Gilley and to see how *My Family Financial Miracle* can work for you, please visit www.myfamilyfinancial-miracle.com.

Family Financial Miracle Representative Registry

To find a local Family Financial Representative to help you, please visit www.FFMRegistry.com

The Family Financial Miracle Representative Registry is a collection of highly knowledgeable advisors working in all fifty states.

Family Financial Miracle Representatives have been specially trained in the understanding of Equity Indexed Universal Life, specifically IRS codes 7702 and 72(e) and their impact on designing the properly structured maximum efficient life insurance contract.

These highly trained representatives can assist clients in accomplishing their immediate needs. Additional expertise is found in the area of finding money the client may be spending unknowingly and/or unnecessarily so that the client can increase contributions to their accumulated assets while at the same time maintain or improve their current lifestyle.

No Obligation Free Analysis Request Form

☐ Yes! I want to find out how I can make my own Family Financial Miracle. I would like a Family Financial Miracle Representative contact me so I can receive my free, no obligation Family Financial Miracle analysis. I understand that I will not be asked to buy anything or pressured to commit to a life insurance contract during this meeting. I also understand that by sending in my contact information, I will be contacted by a live agent in my area to discuss My Family Financial Miracle and the financial solutions it provides.

Please print and use black ink for readability.

Name: _____

Address: _____

City: _____ State: _____ Zip: _____

Best phone to reach you: _____

Email: _____

Best time to call: _____

We will never trade, rent, sell, or abuse your contact or personal information. By giving us your personal contact information, you are giving us permission to have a Family Financial Miracle Representative contact you.

To help the Family Financial Miracle Representative more effectively help you, please tell us about you. This information will be held in *strict confidence*.

Age _____

Occupation _____

Annual income _____

Your greatest financial concern _____

Do you own your home? _____ Approx mortgage balance_____

Do you own your own business? _____ If yes, what type? _____

How did you learn about My Family Financial Miracle?_____

_____

Please fax, mail or visit us online at www.MyFamilyFinancialMiracle.com/analysis and fill out the form available for you there.

Fax: 757-424-8902 or E-mail: info@myfamilyfinancialmiracle.com
Mailing address: Family Financial Miracle, LLC, 1407 Stephanie Way, Suite B, Chesapeake, VA 23320